Page 9--introduction

Page 15---Prologue

Page 21 --- Chapter 1

Page 29 ---Chapter 2

Page 32--- Chapter 3

Page 50--- Chapter 4

Page 52--- Chapter 5

Page 55--- Chapter 6

Page 56--- Chapter 7

Page 58--- Chapter 8

Page 60--- Chapter 9

Page 70--- Chapter 10

Page 73----------------------------- ---------------------------Chapter 11

Page 78--- Chapter 12

Page 82--- Chapter 13

Page 85--- Chapter 14

Page 87--- Chapter 15

Page 101--- Chapter 16

Page 108--- Chapter 17

Page 113--- Chapter 18

Page 118--- Chapter 19

Page 130--- Chapter 20

As a long-time activist for and on behalf of the African Descent Community around the world, my focus has been to raise the consciousness of our people and to expose the wicked machinations and diabolical deeds of our enemies, historically, present day and of course what they continue to plan against us and the rest of humanity to destroy our future.

For these activities I have had to pay a tremendously high price by being evil spoken of.

I have never complained because the scripture in the Bible says, "struggle is ordained" and "Hard trials are necessary to establish truth" , so over the years I have continued to smile in the face of the enemy.

My continued pledge to all of you who have followed my activities and listened to and have been moved by my recital of the life giving teachings of Mr. E - as taught by The Minister, is that as long as I have breath in my body I will never stop working on behalf of the masses of our African People regardless of the opposition.

I intend to live but if necessary die with my boots on for the truth and the total liberation of our Beautiful Brown Hu*(e)*man *(hue = dark - man = race)* Beings of African Descent.

I have fought long and hard.

I don´t call myself an artist, I don´t call myself an author. I call myself the luxury of being independent from the rest of the world. I am Afro-Centric.

Sometimes I gonna use the F-Word in this book, because racism does not deserve it better.

I met Kidson @ the young age of 23. When we got in touch we had an immediate deep connection on a brotha-hood level. That Gentleman from Ghana taught me a lesson: "Where ever you go in life, think "BLACK!" Expect the worse and you will never ever get disappointed.

I do not wanna die knowing I gave racism a change to establish. When I leave I know I did everything I wanted to do. - and I did it my way.

If I could dream of a better world, where all my brothaz could live a life away from racism, why couldn't I make this dream come true.

Introduction

Scare me and I swear to your fuckin' Piggy Pink Skin Complexion -"God": " Is that all you bring to the fuckin' table?"

*They used to beat me up ever since I was a little tiny child with a belt - age approximately 4 years old, my parents let me stand naked in a corner for several hours, they let me sleep with a sheer plastic bag as my cover in a bath tup - naked, they let me lick the floor -of the apartment with my tongue, they let me stand on one foot for several hours - naked, my father burned my penis -with his cigarette, my mother let me eat raw meat, she used to beat my naked body with her wooden hair-brush, she took my head to smash it several times against a wall in our apartment, she used to kick me as a child like a little football through the entrance hall of the apartment, one day the door smashed wide open and in walked my mother to grap me"her son (age 6 years old)" to pull me into the kitchen -she started to lighten the gas stove and began to burn a part of my hand, she let me eat a bucket full of honey - of course I vomit and since that day - unable to enjoy honey. **I decided to run away from them @ the age of 7. I started to knock on other foreign people doors** and told them a story - just to get shelter. Later they put me into a foster home, where another nightmare started - the nightmare of fuckin' Piggy Pink Racism. They were telling me my nose is ugly, they were telling me my hair is strange, they were telling my lips are too big, they were calling me ever since: A Nigger, a dirty monkey, a negro, the most ugliest human being the Lord has ever created, they were calling me a boy from the jungle.*

Whoever is reading this book and tries to threaten me, I do not fear anything on planet earth.

This message goes out to all 95er (95% Uncle Tom) and also to all you racist bitch ass motherfuckers, who hide their racist attitude by placing their dicks between those legs of an Uncle Tom Woman. Do me a favour read with open eyes and understand me clearly.

I have 0% Uncle Tom DNA in my body, my year of Being a Conscious Man of African Descent, started in 2003-November - it means to you racist motherfuckers, I am officially a threat. I handle racism unapologetically, the way racism needs to be handled, I handle Uncle Tom People the way they need to be handled - to keep them at a distance and enjoy the show when everything is about to collapse. All I say then: "NONE OF MY BUSINESS!!

I address this message directly to a hair dresser named Pascual! How can he be a racist, if he gave a woman of African Descent a Kiss on her cheek and hugged her. How can he be a racist if he gave me money after I did my internship in his Barber Shop. Answer: Racism has no emotions.

When I went to Pascual to get my hair done an employee of his asked me for a favor to go just around the corner to buy a little snack for everybody. **Pascual:** "Yes, let this Nigger walk around for us....did someone burned you or why is your skin so dark!" I was sixteen @ that time. Seven years later, I transformed myself into an activist to kill the unaesthetic of Piggy Pink People by studying their wicked history, their evil psyche and killing "White Supremacy". I became a nightmare for every Police Officer in New York, in Laguna Beach, in Aachen and in London. Whoever approaches me on that level needs to understand, I am the biggest nightmare on planet earth, they gonna remember me for the rest of their fucking unaesthetic, meaningless life.

The very last situation I needed to handle was in London on 2009 December, all I can say is, everything was in a public space and no one from the Piggy Pink Race came to support her, while I was telling that whore off.

Racism needs to be destroyed. These people need to be beaten up on a daily level. She did not refer the N-Word to me, but a word that was not really nice.

I am not on planet earth to feel sorry, for any Piggy Pink or Uncle Tom. I live unapologetically my life and not any Uncle Tom People expectations nor Piggy Pink Society submissive behaviour. Am I arrogant? It seems like! Do you date outside of your race? I am too educated not to do that anymore. My African Descent brain fuckz with the very world best, (not 2nd best) people in the universe to decode your Piggy Pink Racist world and to destroy your post slavery trauma. Any additional questions Mr Racist Piggy Pink, if yes, ask your father, sorry maybe your mother fucked another dude and your so-called Daddy is not that, what your mother told you.

With best regards
....XXX...

P.S.:

If you read my book, whether you are an Uncle Tom, A Piggy Pink Racist, you should know my brain fuckz only on factz to decode every aspects of racism. If you consider to name me as the author of the book a racist, then be kind enough and show me , when, where and how did I practice any racist act towards your unhealthy looking Piggy Pink Skin complexion. If you fuckin´ with me on that topic, please bring only factz to the table - Piggy Pink, Uncle Tom and everybody who is sexually dealing ($$$$$) with a racist Piggy Pink Partner and lives with the idea his/her Piggy Pink is 0% a racist.

I declared officially war to destroy the devil a long time ago. Your time is over. You are dealing with me, that equals the biggest African American nightmare for all, who keeps "WHITE SUPREMACY" alive.
I am handsome, rich, eccentric, afro-centric, sophisticated and choose to live a life completely different from the rest of the boring normal world. I can´t fight racism with a Piggy Pink on my side or an Uncle Tom follower of your Piggy Pink believe system, who sees me as an option to get to something.

Goodbye Racism!
and
Welcome Aesthetic Life!

Prologue

Why am I doing this book? For first, very simple I am not a 95er (95%, prefer to maintain the situation as an uncle Tom), When I see a brown skin I feel attracted to and I am really proud to be a part of the African (conscious) community. Although I am aware of those problems within the unconscious community, whether they do not know who they really are or they made -I guess so - one day, subconsciously the decision to hate themselves as people originated from Africa or they need to maintain the holy peace within a mix race household. There are plenty of other reasons, even financially how to survive in this cruel world. Some make the decision to serve as prostitutes under the roof of a so-called partnership: Boyfriend & Girlfriend, Wife & Husband, Side Chick & Sugar Daddy, direct sex vs. a Chanel (Jewish company who consider blacks as liquid money) bag. Every Brotha who sees a Sista with an ugly gentleman understands the game. It´s all about how to survive. We Brothaz had less power so we silently agree, the ugly looking guy with the pinkish skin complexion provides the money and her real love, that comes from the heart belongs to her real boyfriend/husband. Everything else is an arrangement to survive.

Every Sista understands the game if she sees a Brotha in fancy clothes, expansive Air Jordans and an overweight woman with a Piggy Pink skin complexion. She is providing him with the opportunity to get his papers, that he can stay in a European country.

We must come together one day as one powerful force under the roof of the least dominator, which is our wonderful dark skin complexion. Man must become **GENTLEMAN** again & Women must develop themselves into **sophisticated LADIES**, where we Men have a goal to live for. What is a real **GENTLEMAN**, without a LADY on his side? I do not talk thugz and bitches, what I say as a **GENTLEMAN of African Descent**, we must learn to dress properly again, talk and act without noises in front of a real **LADY** and accept the situation to live for a long period of time alone.

We must understand and see our situation in the African Community as a broken legacy done by these Piggy Pink Slave Masters (their history is written in blood all over the planet and stored in several archives around the globe) and that these evil racist people are never going to fix us up. We must start within ourselves, our household, within our

neighbourhood.

The time came in my life *(in these days I know every Brotha from the conscious community went through that)*, where I made the decision not to obey to all those unwritten rules, when it comes to racism. I was willing to die for my strong opinion because I knew I was right. That gave me the unlimited power to kill the Piggy Pink Society, with an upper arrogant attitude. Every time a Police Officer would stop me in my car, I would say to myself:"O.k., let´s play the game!"

I had nothing then my aesthetic belief system, a skill how to use language, a skill how to act through body language, that still makes me appear to them as the biggest nightmare. I would step out of my car and scream: "I understand the game, place a bullet in my head!" I was fearless and @ the same time I knew, it ´s better to change the game. So, I made the decision not to drive a car by my own anymore!- (wisdom).

My book is all about to change into the conscious mind of what we really are. And not what the d-evil taught us.

My book is not for those 95er (95% uncle Toms), my book is not for stupid thugz, my book is not for the formerly known "WHITE RACE!"-

Piggy Pink (*their history is written in blood all over the planet and stored in several archives around the globe*), my book is not for women of African Descent, who has something sexually going on with a Piggy Pink (their history is written in blood all over the planet and stored in several archives around the globe),

all you guys, I gonna quote my mentor: "Well, let them live in LA-LA Fantasy Land, that everything is alright. Just stay away from them and when the bubble is about to burst, it´s none of your business, because it has a no deeper effect on your aesthetic life. They can not even reach you for help." **-thank you, my dear mentor, Boyce.**

This book is alone dedicated for that 5 % who wants to make a drastic change in their life and need a guide, what is really going on, subconsciously created by these evil Piggy Pink People *(their history is written in blood all over the planet and stored in several archives around the globe)*!

I am the Author and for sure, I am not gonna use my real name.

Chapter 1

Aestheticism is a deeper sense of spirituality without giving it the label of White Jesus, Allah, or Buddha. For many thousands of years, when there was not the "Lord, the God or Allah *(which means God in another language)!*

We as the first hu*(e)*man *(hue = dark - man = people)* beings on planet earth had an aesthetic belief system to live by certain rules of a beautiful mind setting based on logical science.

That specific frame of a supreme understanding was important to get things done, that specific organize mindset was important to be organized in groups *(family, friends, etc.)*

The Christian *(Piggy Pink People)* religion considers their **"God"** as a mystery. **The Father, The Son, The Holy Ghost = One single "God!"**

They confirm he has been made like him *(the Piggy Pink Race).*

Their "God" of Christianity brought us:

Problems, hate, dividing, no equal rights, no justice.

Christianity

+

Slavery
Suffering
Apartheid/Segregation
Cops Killing "BLACKS"
BLUE - KLUX - KLAN

=

DEATH

Is there a higher supreme Piggy Pink **"God?"** If yes, why let "God" the Holocaust happened?"

Is there a supreme good **"God?"** If yes, why let **"God"** *(the Christianity)* 400 years of brutal slavery took place among our Brothaz & Sistaz of African Descent?

Is there a supreme **"God?"** If yes, why do we have: "Cops killing blacks?"

The Aesthetic is a belief system of righteousness! The teaching of the d-evil race, Piggy Pink People (their history is written in blood all over the planet and stored in several archives around the globe) is over.

My Brothaz and Sistaz of African Descent are the victims of Christianity. *(95 % of our African community prefers to play Uncle Tom)*. The African Community is deaf and blind, I am going to prove with my book, that we were born with the six sense of a deeper fantastic, working spirituality. rhythm, inner peace, inner beauty, that equals in an extraordinary frame.

While Piggy Pink People *(their history is written in blood all over the planet and stored in several archives around the globe)* were living in caves, we Beautiful Brown Hu*(e)*man *(hue = dark - man = race)* Beings were ruling over the planet for over 66 trillions of years, we were dressed in silk. Beauty and aesthetic from the inside is a part of our DNA, that makes us ultra sensitive as the original hu*(e)*man *(hue = dark - man = race)* beings on planet earth.

Example:

Piggy Pink People *(their history is written in blood all over the planet and stored in several archives around the globe)* has not the equivalent, who can ever sing like the Soul Diva Whitney Houston.

There is no one from the Piggy Pink Race *(their history is written in blood all over the planet and stored in several archives around the globe)*, who could ever perform like Michael Jackson and sing like the King of Pop.

There is no one from the dominant society of the formerly known "White Race" *(their history is written in blood all over the planet and stored in several archives around the globe)*, who can play tennis like Serena Williams *(uncle Tom)* and win Wimbledon while she was pregnant.

While Piggy Pink People (their history is written in blood all over the planet and stored in several archives around the globe) were living in caves, we Beautiful Brown Hu*(e)*man *(hue = dark - man = race)* Beings were ruling over the planet for over 66 trillions of years, we were dressed in silk. Beauty and aesthetic from the inside is a part of our DNA, that makes us ultra sensitive as the original hu(e)man *(hue = dark - man = race)* beings on planet earth.

There is nobody from the Piggy Pink Race (their history is written in blood all over the planet and stored in several archives around the globe), who is able to play Golf and win like Tiger Woods and is considered the "Master of Golf!"

The so-called better "White Race", their true skin complexion is Piggy Pink *(their history is written in blood all over the planet and stored in several archives around the globe)* is not able to become a "God" of basketball like Michael "Air" Jordan or Magic Johnson.

> **a deeper African spirit connected to something bigger in the universe.**

> **Something has been given by mother nature, a connection to mother earth as the first hu(e)mans (hue = dark - man = race) on planet earth, that the Piggy Pink - Race fear.**

> **We are the original people on planet earth and every other race comes from our DNA** *(Asians, Piggy Pink People, Native Americans, Indians).*

> **We Beautiful Brown Hu*(e)*man** *(hue = dark - man = race)* **Beings of African Descent, were on the planet, long before the so-called better "White Race"** *(their history is written in blood all over the planet and stored in several archives around the globe).*

Everything comes out of the womb of an African Descent Queen. She is the Mother of civilization she gave birth to all those children, who enslaved us and still fighting us. The so-called **"God"** of Christianity, the so-called creator, that does not exist, was used by the d-evil to trick our mindset. Who is that Piggy Pink Christianity **"God",** that has been used to enslave my Brothaz & Sistaz, did **"God"** say it: **"Name a ship after my son Jesus and bring slaves to America?"** The most important question is: **"Why do we believe in such a wicked "God?"** Do we Brothaz and Sistaz of African Descent wanna admirer such a **"God"**, who did not stop the cruel slavery holocaust against Beautiful Brown Hu*(e)*man Beings *(hue = dark - man = race)* of African Descent?

The darker the skin complexion the more sensitive each individual of African Descent. Our highly sensitive African Descent Hu*(e)*man Being race is based on the six sense, in general. Who is that **"God"**, who claimed to found us in the jungle with a bone in our hair and nose? Our so-called Black people *(95% prefers to play uncle Tom)* are following an enigma, that has never been existing. We Beautiful Brown Hu*(e)*mans *(hue = dark - man = race)* on planet earth and everything else came out from the womb of the Beautiful Brown Hu*(e)*man *(hue = dark - man = race)* woman, the Mother of civilization. Every life comes from the *(hue)* dark. The d-evil has no love for his hu*(e)*man *(hue = dark - man = race)* mother. So does not the majority of all those 95er *(95% Uncle Tom Brothaz & Sistaz)*. Every Uncle Tom *(95% of the African Descent Community)*, claim how much they love their mother, but when it comes to show real love, they try to deny their Beautiful Brown Hu*(e)*man *(hue = dark - man = race)* Being identity. They fall for the miseducation by the d-evil.

The Piggy Pink Race *(their history is written in blood all over the planet and stored in several archives around the globe)* will never teach them, who they really are! My dear Brothaz & Sistaz, if you know the time and present time of your inner aesthetic soul, that we are able to produce true magic *(like **Michael Jackson, Whitney Houston, Michael "Air" Jordan, Magic Johnson, Tiger Woods, Serena and Venus Williams ...etc**)*, tell me who seeks to follow the evil game of the wicked Piggy Pink Race. And not the inner aesthetic feelings of your true African spirit?

Is the Piggy Pink *(their history is written in blood all over the planet and stored in several archives around the globe)* **"God"** a good spirit or a tool to destroy the world

of **"None White"** people? According to the "Bible" -
Christianity is the religion of the slave master. You are
made to believe that the true "God" is Christ. Do you
know to live aesthetic is the truth? Do you know
Piggy Pink People *(their history is written in blood all over
the planet and stored in several archives around the globe)*
try all the time to destroy the aesthetic by killing the
aesthetic musician Michael Jackson, Whitney
Houston, Dr Martin Luther King, Brotha Malcolm X,
Steven Biko....the Piggy Pink racist history is written
in blood all over the planet and stored in several
archives around the globe. They killed Asians, they
killed Native Americans, they killed Aborigines
(original hu(e)man (hue = dark - man = race) in Australia.

The truth of an own Kingdom of Aesthetic for
Beautiful Brown Hu*(e)*man *(hue= dark - man = race)*
Beings, is in the power to watch deep inside of his
soul, create an aesthetic circle and obey only to those
rules.

Chapter 2

Aesthetic examples

No Alcohol *(product of the d-evil. He provides the alcohol, that makes you ill and takes your hard earned money to send his wicked children to private school, while your family is suffering)*.

Hard work to become independent financially.
No sneakers, no sagging, dress only proper, because we were dressed in silk, while the d-evil was living in caves.

Do sport. Good for your inner stability.
Read as much books as you can *(self development)*!

Study our African ancient history.
Do not send your children to a wicked Piggy Pink *(their history is written in blood all over the planet and stored in several archives around the globe)* school system, the d-evil will not teach them, who we Beautiful Brown Hu*(e)*man *(hue = dark - man = race)* Beings really are. The d-evil is never going to teach you, that his wicked Piggy Pink Race *(their history is written in blood all over the planet and stored in several archives around the globe)* has been around for only 6.000 years and our ancestors for 66 trillion years.

My dear Brothaz and Sistaz,

if you only know the present situation of your inner aesthetic, that is able to transform your soul to produce true magic *(like Whitney Houston, Michael Jackson, Michael Jordan, Tiger Woods, Singer Prince ...etc)* you could change your life from the unaesthetic Piggy Pink *(their history is written in blood all over the planet and stored in several archives around the globe)* world, into something sophisticated, with a deeper touch of wonderful aesthetic, that no Piggy Pink *(their history is written in blood all over the planet and stored in several archives around the globe)* could ever do. Why seek to follow Piggy Pink People *(their history is written in blood all over the planet and stored in several archives around the globe)* and their evil doing? And not the inner deep beauty of an African Soul? Is the Piggy Pink "God" *(their history is written in blood all over the planet and stored in several archives around the globe)* a good spirit or a tool to destroy the world of "None White" people?

Dis-functional Piggy Pink religion *(their history is written in blood all over the planet and stored in several archives around the globe)* pushes you into a direction, where a mystery "God" has given you that Piggy Pink *(their history is written in blood all over the planet and stored in several archives around the globe) (their history is written in blood all over the planet and stored in several archives around the globe)* of common sense to let you stuck in his racist mind frame. If you go deeper you see, that their religion had only being used to conquer, destroy, to kill and enslave everything, that is none Piggy Pink *(their history is written in blood all over the planet and stored in several archives around the globe),* the reality of Piggy Pink "God" *(their history is written in blood all over the planet and stored in several archives around the globe)* has been a mystery ever since.

There must come a day where all hu*(e)*man beings *(hue = dark - man = race)* should come together as Beautiful Brown Hu*(e)*man *(hue =dark - man = race)* Beings, driven by the aesthetic from the inside.

How can we Beautiful Brown Hu*(e)*mans *(hue = dark - man = race)* serve a Piggy Pink *(their history is written in blood all over the planet and stored in several archives around the globe)* "God", that were used to enslave us and is still used to manipulate our beautiful spirit.

My Brothaz and Sistaz of African Descent are worse off, if it comes to the reality of Piggy Pink People *(their history is written in blood all over the planet and stored in several archives around the globe)* "God!" The whole world is looking for the coming of the Holy Lord! Thousands of years the d-evil has been blinded us by the reality of their so called "Jesus & God."

"God" = Bible = Christianity = **Their history is written in blood all over the planet and stored in several archives around the globe.**

Chapter 3

An Aesthetic Believe System to believe in the supreme beauty what has been implemented in us ever since by mother nature. That gives us guidance into inspiration, greatness in service for the aesthetic.
The evil working of the **Devil** must come to an end!
If we people of African Descent consider the destruction of the d-evil, how would the world look like?
The Piggy Pink world *(their history is written in blood all over the planet and stored in several archives around the globe)*, is a wicked place, whether you an as Uncle Tom *(95% of the African Descent Community)* agree or not. In order not to follow his plans to destruct people of African Descent, give the world over to the righteousness of the supreme aesthetic.
The 1st teacher, 2nd teacher, 3rd teacher ...etc.!

You need to understand how we were made slaves by using the cross symbol **(+)** of Christianity. How we were made: Blind, deaf and dump by Piggy Pink Racist *(their history is written in blood all over the planet and stored in several archives around the globe)* society, by using "God" as a believe system.

Do you understand Brothaz & Sistaz why we must return to ourselves to approach our hu*(e)*man *(hue = dark - man = race)* kind? We must give up our slave names by our slave masters, except the name of the Aesthetic. The Aesthetic teaches us also to give up all evil doing and practices and to do righteousness or otherwise we gonna be destroyed again by racist Piggy Pink *(their history is written in blood all over the planet and stored in several archives around the globe)* society. If we submit completely to the Aesthetic, we are going to receive the teaching, we gonna live an extraordinary life. The Kingdom loves Beautiful Brown Hu*(e)*man *(hue = dark - man = race)* Beings, because Aesthetic is a part of our DNA.

We from the Aesthetic came to guide you into an aesthetic life. You gonna be successful and see the year after.

Nothing of Piggy Pink People *(their history is written in blood all over the planet and stored in several archives around the globe)* man kind will last, if we people of African

Descent takes over leadership. We are going succeed like Tiger Woods, Michael Jackson, Singer Prince, Whitney Huston, Michael "Air" Jordan ... etc!

Christianity was only organized by Piggy Pink *(their history is written in blood all over the planet and stored in several archives around the globe)* to enslave **"All None White people."** I bear to witness it has also enslaved our people in the United States. The aesthetic is our salvation, it removes fear, anger and it brings peace to our mind that we can find something in it to distance ourselves from Piggy Pink *(their history is written in blood all over the planet and stored in several archives around the globe)*. As soon our people are aware of their own inner aesthetic that we have been the original first hu*(e)*man beings *(hue = dark - man = race)* on planet earth, we find peace, positive energy and heaven in the Aesthetic. We are the original material on earth, from our African Descent DNA comes all human, the African Woman gave birth to our No.1 enemy the wicked Piggy Pink Race *(their history is written in blood all over the planet and stored in several archives around the globe)*, she gave birth to Asians, she gave birth to Native Americans, she gave birth to Indians ... etc! We have been so long separated from each other as Beautiful Brown Hu*(e)*man *(hue = dark - man = race)* Beings, that we lost the knowledge of each other. Even today the slave master is keeping the secret of truth that might teach us to come together. They are our open enemies. The so-called Goddess the African Queen, who is able to give birth to all colours.

After his conquest of his "Black" enemies, the world will recognize him as evil alone because throughout the world Piggy Pink racist history is written in blood!

There is no bigger problem to solve for us than unity among Beautiful Brown Hu(e)man Beings of African Descent. They like deaf "Black" Uncle Tom people without asking to deep questions. And if you dare to dig deep into their wicked history *(their history is written in blood all over the planet and stored in several archives around the globe)*, they consider to destroy your families life or even kill you like brotha Malcolm X.

Uncle Tom People have lost all love of **"Self"** and kind. And they have gone out in making love to their enemies. They do not want any aesthetic blessing, unless their Piggy Pink *(their history is written in blood all over the planet and stored in several archives around the globe)*, get any blessing, too.

Beautiful Brown Hu*(e)*man *(hue = dark - man = race)* Beings should not have any fear, only the fear of the aesthetic, that might happen, if you refuse to live something wonderful. By all means, Beautiful Brown Hu(e)man *(hue = dark - man = race)* Beings, must be separated from the racist Piggy Piggy humankind.

In order, we can lead a Beautiful Brown Hu(e)man *(hue = dark - man = race)* Being Kingdom of Aesthetic or go to take you back into slavery. African Descent People we have no home, we can call our own. They have helped the d-evil to win a free country. But Beautiful Brown Hu(e)man Beings have nothing for themselves. The Aesthetic will come to give them, what is rightfully theirs.

What is the Aesthetic? It is a belief system to act in a righteous way to free you from the hand of your slave master. The Aesthetic will give you the power to overcome your enemies. With the help of the aesthetic belief system, you gonna have inner power like a lion to do for yourself. You are going to understand how to feed your family and child.

That specific frame of a beautiful mindset is going to change your life into sophistication forever. If you live by all those rules to escape racism, your inner life is going to change.

Do not forget, that every Piggy Pink *(their history is written in blood all over the planet and stored in several archives around the globe)* is going to fight you, because of the reason the devil is going to lose power over you *(ourselves)*. They going to believe we are not real Aesthetic Beautiful Brown Hu*(e)*man *(hue = dark - man = race)* Beings. Because we do not look and talk like **"Black People"** should talk and look like. Remember the aesthetic is not about a look, the aesthetic belief system goes beyond looks. It is a part of our ancient African Descent DNA for over 66 trillions of years. They gonna fight us, they gonna think we have a different way to approach life. Piggy Pink People (their history is written in blood all over the planet and stored in several archives around the globe) is going to hate us. Because we are going to confront them, only by factz, that these people are evil *(their history is written in blood all over the planet and stored in several archives around the globe)*! We do not need weapons to destroy the d-evil. Our educated mind is the force to protect us from the unaesthetic world. They gonna try to fool us, they gonna try to trick us: "We are actually not bad people." We gonna say: ***"Your history has been written in blood and is still a witness of violence and hate."*** Piggy Pink Supremacy *(formerly white supremacy)* *(their history is written in blood all over the planet and stored in several archives around the globe)*!

- because Oncle Tom and Piggy Pink *(their history is written in blood all over the planet and stored in several archives around the globe)* themselves believe, that they are superior, because they gave themselves the label **"WHITE"**...it stands for every positive aspect of life. You wear **WHITE** during a **wedding ceremony**, you make peace by showing the **white flag**. When a race has got that silly mentality, like Adolf Hitler and needed to witness during the Olympic games, that Jesse Owens, an African American, kicked out the organs by running faster than these Piggy Pink Competitors *(their history is written in blood all over the planet and stored in several archives around the globe)* Adolf Hitler was outraged. Pushing White Supremacy, that is one of those many reasons, why they would cut off your penis when they'd lynch **"BLACKS"**.

Penis envy = They are afraid of the "Black Man", because of our potency and stronger DNA.

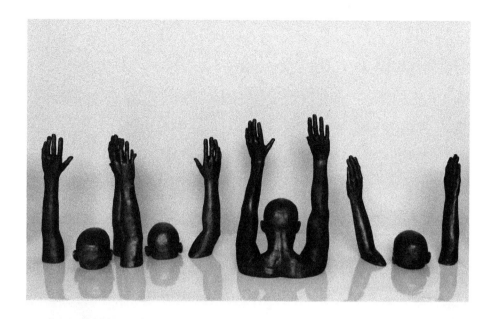

If you look @ a Beautiful Brown Hu(e)man (hue = dark - man = race) Being of African Descent, you are looking @ a real strong Beautiful Man. Piggy Pink People *(their history is written in blood all over the planet and stored in several archives around the globe)* want to be heavyweight champion of the world, they can't find a Piggy Pink *(their history is written in blood all over the planet and stored in several archives around the globe)*. We were not allowed to play golf, all of a sudden there is a **"Tiger"** in the **"Woods."** He just does not play golf, he is the "Master of Golf." We were not allowed to play tennis. Let one "Black Guy" in, we went to Wimbledon and won the match in 1935. Now, we have Serena Williams (Uncle Tom), the Piggy Pink Race *(their history is written in blood all over the planet and stored in several archives around the globe)*

can't compete with her on a plane field. They let us into athletics, the Piggy Pink race can't run like a Beautiful Brown Hu*(e)*man *(hue = dark - man = race)* Being of African Descent. Whatever field we are in, we dominate it. They are inferior, but Piggy Pink plays superior to hide their inferiority. The problem is, they know we are stronger and better.

Every time a so-called "Black Leader" came to lead us out of the darkness, they consider to kill him. They killed brotha Malcolm X, they killed brotha Dr. Martin Luther King, they killed Patrice Lumumba and they killed brotha Steven Biko....!

Furthermore, they put Nelson Mandela in prison for 27 years. A Piggy Pink *(their history is written in blood all over the planet and stored in several archives around the globe)* admitted, they were slowly poisoning him to destroy his mental faculties, when these evil, devilish, fucking, racist, Piggy Pink People *(their history is written in blood all over the planet and stored in several archives around the globe)*, realize he was no longer a potent force, they let him walk out of Robben Island. Under the illusion of inclusion that racism is going to come to an end, slowly. They started to use him as an Uncle Tom puppet for the world public audience. However his former wife Winnie Mandela a warrior, a Beautiful Brown Queen of African Descent, refused to shake hands with former President Ronald Reagan or Maggie Thatcher, Winnie wouldn't bow, but Nelson would bow down. These wicked Piggy Pink People *(their history is written in blood all over the planet and stored in several archives around the globe)*, they make the decision to embrace Nelson, they presented him to the world as an Uncle Tom of forgive'ness.

Brotha Malcolm X did not consider to dance to those rules, brotha Dr Martin Luther King did not consider to dance to those rules, Brotha Steven Biko did not consider to dance to those rules and bow down. What does it tell us, my dear Brothaz and Sistaz?

The Aesthetic does not dance and bow down to the d-evil, we are soldiers. We must understand that the d-evil never fought in Africa, one-on-one, they came to divide us from one another. We people from the Kingdom are going to set the record straight that everything is "BLACK&WHITE." We people from the Aesthetic are no longer asking for acceptance. We are not going to ask you anymore to love us. What we say is goodbye to the racist label "BLACK", that you gave us, when we were only seen as merchandise to trade with. We are members of the Aesthetic following a true principle of self-discipline and principles that we are the very first and original hu(e)man (hue = dark - man) race on planet earth. And that the African descent woman is the Mother of civilization. She gave birth to the race that is fighting her.

We are students of wisdom and life long learning, we dedicate our time to study your cruel Piggy Pink history *(their history is written in blood all over the planet and stored in several archives around the globe)*.

We dedicate our aesthetic taste to dress in an absolute clear sophisticated way, the reason is: "While the so-called "White Man" was living in caves, we were dressed in silk and already had a civilization running. We know that all Piggy Pink *(their history is written in blood all over the planet and stored in several archives around the globe)* are evil and connected to the devil. So please, do not come around and tell us, you are different because you place your dick inside a "Black Sista" or you swallow from a "Black Brotha." We are able and educated enough to break each individual down as a racist *(Donald Sterling - Syndrome)*.We Beautiful Brown Hu*(e)*man Beings are directly opposed to the original, first hu*(e)*man *(hue = dark - man = race)* beings on planet earth connected to something higher that is bigger than anything on planet earth. The aesthetic is going to reform the African hu*(e)*man *(hue = dark - man = race)* descent, family. Our nature is to be aesthetic and extraordinary sophisticated from the inside.

Chapter 3

Under the belief system of Christianity, the so-called Christians became the most successful people on the planet.

We must understand that most of our African Brothaz&Sistaz do not live by an aesthetic principle that is going to stop, that "White Wash" brain mentality. Take a book and study the history of the d-evil *(their history is written in blood all over the planet and stored in several archives around the globe)* and their present time is still written in blood. The whole Caucasian race is a family of devils.

If you understand that the devil follows only an equation to succeed in his cruelty towards "BLACKS" you are able to decode him immediately. Only understand that math-science equation:

A Piggy Pink Man + A Woman of African Descent = African Descent Baby. "Half-breed!"

A Piggy Pink Woman + A Piggy Pink Man = A Piggy Pink Baby.

These people have proven to be d-evils by intoxicating our mind. Over several centuries, they were able to let us believe we are 2nd class hu*(e)*man (hue = dark - man = race) beings, although we are the original and first race on planet earth. Our enemies greatest desire is the wish that we are remaining asleep. The belief system of the Kingdom of Aesthetic is going to wake our Brothaz and Sistaz up and bring from the subconscious mind the evil of Piggy Pink People (their history is written in blood all over the planet and stored in several archives around the globe).

The Aesthetic is going to send the devil, the Piggy Pink Race (their history is written in blood all over the planet and stored in several archives around the globe) a clear message that their time of oppression is over, because we understand how, the devil works on a longterm equation to reduce our African descent numbers for example: " Cops Killing Blacks or creating the Hi-Virus ... etc.!

We people of African descent are going to stop

to attack the d-evil on an emotional level, we are going to use math science to fix ourselves up. First ourselves as an individual, then our household, then our families and then the whole African Descent Community. If we Beautiful Brown Hu*(e)*man Beings of African Descent follow this aesthetic scheme, those principles by the Kingdom of Aesthetic, that sets us in a superior elegant position, so that the d-evil must give us reparations and return our home continent, Africa, back, in a proper circumstance, like the German gave reparation to the so "Called Jews."

We do not ask the devil to pay each single person money because we know that our Sistaz have nothing better to do, then to go to racist Haute Couture Chanel *(own by Jewish people, who consider: " Blacks as liquid money)* and bring the money straight into the system of Piggy Pink People *(their history is written in blood all over the planet and stored in several archives around the globe)*.

We know that our Brothaz would directly hire the fanciest pin-up Russian beauty/prostitute and waste his money of reparation straight away with the d-evil.

Russian pin-up Beauty: "Actually, I do not date Niggers, but if he is willing enough to pay all....!!!"

If we accept the power of the belief system of the

Aesthetic, we are going to have an universal friendship with our Brothaz and Sistaz additionally a dominant force to stop the d-evil. We know the d-evil is going to prosecute everyone, who is going to help us?

First, we need to have the friendship with our own race, like these Asians and then independence and as a power structure, aesthetic autonomy that leads the democratic affairs of our Beautiful Brown Hu(e)man *(hue = dark - man = race)* Being into an official frame.

Self is the goal for each individual in the Aesthetic world.

Independence & Self guidance of our Aesthetic is the goal. Fear is the worst enemy a Beautiful Brown Hu*(e)*man *(hue = dark - man = race)* Being in the Kingdom of Aesthetic can have. There is no fear necessary if he submits completely to the aesthetic. The d-evil put fear in our parents, when they were little Babies, it's written in their history.

We must have our own peace, what other nations have. Peace can´t come on any other flag, but our own African - Aesthetic. **Our first step is to give back to Piggy Pink** *(their history is written in blood all over the planet and stored in several archives around the globe)* his **"God,"** his **"Pope"** and his **"Name."**

These three chains of slavery that hold us bondage to them. We are immediately free if we walk away from these three foolish things that keep us "White-washed!" The Piggy Pink racist society (their history is written in blood all over the planet and stored in several archives around the globe) will never agree to the belief structure of the Aesthetic, because we stop to believe in them. It is foolish to believe the d-evils religion is made for us. It proofs it had been created to go to war against other countries. "God" has not sent anyone to kill people of African Descent nor requested to name a ship "Jesus" to bring Africans as "BLACK MERCHANDISE"- as slaves to the United States. Piggy Pink *(their history is written in blood all over the planet and stored in several archives around the globe)* sent himself under the excuse of the Holy Lord, their "God."

Piggy Pink: "I am superior from the better race, we found you in the jungle of Africa with a bone in your hair and nose.
If we study the history of the wicked Piggy Pink Race *(their history is written in blood all over the planet and stored in several archives around the globe)* they are on planet earth for **6000 years** *(six thousand)*.
If we study African Descent history we are around since the beginning, of the beginning, of the hu*(e)*man *(hue = dark -man = race)* kind. Although no **"God"** was

around, we were able to consider our Beautiful Brown Hu*(e)*man *(hue = dark - man = race)* Race as a holy spirit.

The Aesthetic is going to judge the Piggy Pink Race *(their history is written in blood all over the planet and stored in several archives around the globe)* between man & man, empire & empire. If we wanna understand the present time we must go to study their wicked history. The Aesthetic must teach the truth about their spiritual blindness. Also, the Aesthetic must teach that our Brothaz and Sistaz can´t walk out of the evil environment created by the devil, without the help of an aesthetic belief system. You see how Beautiful Brown Hu*(e)*man Beings are suffering, you see how your "BLACK MOTHER" is suffering from the filth created by the so-called "BETTER RACE" = THE DEVIL!

Submit to the Aesthetic a belief system for Beautiful Brown Hu*(e)*man *(hue = dark - man = race)* Beings of African Descent! The Aesthetic whoever will serve the beauty of the Kingdom he/she will get his inner reward and will have no fear. Fear is the No.1 enemy for Beautiful Brown Hu*(e)*man *(hue = dark - man = race)* of African Descent, with a greater sense of spirituality.

The Piggy Pink Race (their history is written in blood all over the planet and stored in several archives around the globe) know that his enemies the so-called "BLACKS" have suffered for 450 years, we have been oppressed more than any other human race on planet earth. This fear is the fear of the wicked, fucking slave master. The fear of Piggy Pink people (their history is written in blood all over the planet and stored in several archives around the globe) is going to bring us closer together as an institution. The slave master puts fear in our parents when they were Babies. The inner aesthetic believe system is the only tool that can remove the fear in us. However, it's not going to be removed alone until we submit to the power of our inner spirit. We must remember that inner beauty, means an entire submission to the will of the aesthetic that & that alone is the true way out of the d-evil's hell.

Chapter 4

It is the will of the Aesthetic, that we will know ourselves.

You should know that the so-called Piggy Pink Race *(their history is written in blood all over the planet and stored in several archives around the globe)* was created 6000 years ago. That is not our number. We Beautiful Brown Hu*(e)*man *(hue = dark - man = race)* Beings of African Descent have not really a birth record.

First, love yourself! Love your dark skin complexion. One of the greatest handicap of our Brothaz & Sistaz, that there is no love for themselves, **95% are "WHITE-WASHED"** no love for his or her kind. Just not having love for **"Self"** is the root cause of hate, disunite, disagreement, dislike, fighting and killing one another. How can you request love for your "BLACK RACE" if the "WHITE RACE" is in deep awareness of your self-hate and use it to divide us? Brothaz & Sistaz pretend to love everybody:"I love everybody!" This can't be true. Love of "Self" comes first. The one who loves everybody does not love anyone. This is the none sense teaching of Piggy Pink (their history is written in blood all over the planet and stored in several archives around the globe) "God."

Love yourself and your Beautiful Brown Hu(e)man Beings *(hue = dark - man = race)* of African Descent. Let us love each other as Brothaz & Sistaz as we are the same color under one roof. In this way you and I will never have any trouble. Our brown colour is the best and never try changing its colour. Stay away from inter mixing with your slave master. Love yourself and the rest of the Beautiful Brown Hu(e)man *(hue = dark - man = race)* Being Family. Understand yourself.

We are not **"BLACK!"**

We were named as **"BLACK"** because the Piggy Pink Race *(their history is written in blood all over the planet and stored in several archives around the globe)* saw us as **"BLACK MERCHANDISE"** that can be sold and trade with. We were **"BLACK SLAVE PRODUCTS."** We still have no equals rights on behalf of the dominant Piggy Pink Society (their history is written in blood all over the planet and stored in several archives around the globe)!

Chapter 5

We are Brothaz and Sistaz of African Descent with a dark skin complexion. We are not coloured people, we are not n!ggers, we are not Negroes. We must become aware of our time and power we have in these days, based on the fact the d-evil created the internet (actually it was a Nigerian Scientist, but that is another story).

We went to school, where they do not teach the knowledge of "Ourselves." We go all the time to a school system by our slave master children. The gap of our knowledge of "Self" is our biggest handicap. It blocks us throughout the world. If we do not know our own deep "Self" ancient history, how can we be accepted by people who have a knowledge of "Self?" Are we representing ourselves as "N!GGERS & BLACKS" or as sophisticated HU(E)MAN (HU(E) = DARK - MAN = RACE) BEINGS in the ancient history of: "We were the very first hu(e)man on earth."

VIRGINIAN LUXURIES.

It will prove that separation is the only solution for all former slaves in the United States. -When she named her citizen. You must understand that we are mocked 24/7. It is a disgrace for us to be only a servant part. If we accept our inner aesthetic soul.

What are we waiting for? The destruction? Who are you waiting for to teach the knowledge of "Self"? The Devil? Your former slave master? Sugar Daddy Donald Sterling? The Piggy Pink Society will never do anything for us. If the so-called "BLACKS" keeps believing in "WHITE" and lives under the roof of modern slavery not to accept, who he is, we from the aesthetic world must understand that he /she is a dumb. The slave master has the interest to keep the blind - blind, the deaf- deaf! Even the idea alone to make you conscious of what the d-evil really stands for, that you might be free an independent thinker like Brotha Malcolm X, who was able to decode the d-evil

The d-evil knows you are dumb enough to accept his truth of an independent thinker. The whole western atmosphere belongs to darker people. Piggy Pink *(their history is written in blood all over the planet and stored in several archives around the globe)* will never teach our children the true history of African Descent. The knowledge of our inner aesthetic, spirituality of being the first hu*(e)*man *(hue = dark - man = race)* on planet earth, the creator of all humankind. This limited understanding of the Piggy Pink Race *(their history is written in blood all over the planet and stored in several archives around the globe)*, makes it absolute against his rules to honour & respect our beautiful race of African Descent.

The Piggy Pink Race *(their history is written in blood all over the planet and stored in several archives around the globe)* has been around ever since for the purpose to destroy our peace as well our children future.

They have destroyed 850 million people of African Descent since they have been on our planet.

Chapter 6

The Aesthetic is going to become a new belief system for our Brothaz & Sistaz of African Descent, we are going to see the change now by using new patterns to succeed the game. We must have a new common understanding of our African Descent heritage. We are not here anymore to please the d-evil and his Uncle Tom followers. Because we will never be loved and seen as equal hu(e)man *(hue = dark - man = race)* beings by the d-evil. Whatever the aesthetic spirit desires we are going to serve that specific upscale beauty.

Piggy Pink People (their history is written in blood all over the planet and stored in several archives around the globe): "Black Man" we found you & taught your nation civilization. Our place in the sun to accept our own hu*(e)*man *(hue = dark - man = race)* kind as the first race on planet earth makes sense. We need to stop to love these wicked Piggy Pink People *(their history is written in blood all over the planet and stored in several archives around the globe)*. Let all 95er *(95% Uncle Tom)* deal with them. We from the aesthetic world are too sophisticated and conscious of who they really are. We remember when King George of England refuses autonomy for the Americans. Brother USA fought against the biggest force on the planet. The Piggy Pink Race(their history is written in blood all over the planet and stored in several archives around the globe) in America were willing to die for freedom, justice and equal rights. War is not the goal! We Brothaz and Sistaz must come to the truth of our own identity. We are the original people of the planet for billions of years. We must understand that we are directly linked to our own deep inner spirit and do not need to serve a Piggy Pink *(their history is written in blood all over the planet and stored in several archives around the globe)* **"God!"** - to find the answer of a deeper understanding. We must come together under one roof and punish the d-evil with ignorance by returning to our own deep aesthetic spirit.

Chapter 7

Who is the original race? There are millions who have no idea. From her, the African Queen came all humankind, Racist Piggy Pink People *(their history is written in blood all over the planet and stored in several archives around the globe)*, Asians, Native Americans. We have an unending history of our past. And a limited one for the Piggy Pink People Race *(their history is written in blood all over the planet and stored in several archives around the globe)*. The history teaches us that the planet has been populated by Beautiful Brown Hu*(e)*man *(hue = ark - man = race)* Beings ever since the world was created. However, the Piggy Pink Race does not take themselves beyond 6000 *(six thousand)* years. The Piggy Pink Race does not owe any part on the planet.

If you understand that, there is not any big challenge to deal with these evil people. We take it further by understanding that Piggy Pink are not even their own creators. It is time to know, who you are after 450 years of slavery in racist Piggy Pink (their history is written in blood all over the planet and stored in several archives around the globe) America. It has never been the Piggy Pink People (their history is written in blood all over the planet and stored in several archives around the globe) intention to give us great knowledge of our true African Descent identity. We are brought to the United States only for one single purpose to do the slavery work.

As Beautiful Brown Hu(e)man *(hue = dark - man = race)* beings we must become producers and agree to do for ourselves. How many fashion brands do we owe? Very few.

How many fortunes 500 companies we name our own? Very simple answer: "Zero!" We give all the money out of our pocket to the slave master. Where is our shoe factory, where is our premium car brand?

However, we want equality with the racist Piggy Pink *(their history is written in blood all over the planet and stored in several archives around the globe)* nation. Let's make ourselves equal by producing and selling our aesthetic products. We are begging the slave master for a job, begging him for a recognition to see us as equal. Let us be honest with ourselves. We can´t be equal with the slave master until we owe, what the slave master owns.

We can not be equal until we have an education curriculum as the slave master.

An aesthetic is someone who keeps his inner balance in peace on the first level and secondly, transforms it into a sophisticated behaviour by accepting and respecting his Brothaz & Sistaz - even these 95% Uncle Tom People. He serves only his Kingdom of Aesthetic and never the unaesthetic. The unsophisticated must be kept outside of his world, that he is able to serve the supreme beauty.

Chapter 8

We do not depend on Piggy Pink *(their history is written in blood all over the planet and stored in several archives around the globe)*, because we do for ourselves, we do not depend on 95er *(95% are Uncle Tom)* because we do not allow them into our circle of sophistication, base on the fact they do not speak and understand our view regarding the racist d-evil. They might see us as an option to get to a financially better life. We need to consider to tell them, that a sexual arrangement under the illusion of a relationship (Sugar Daddy & Sugar Baby/Prostitution) is an easier option.

Unaesthetic + Unaesthetic = Gambling! An unaesthetic bubble that is going to burst one day. None of our business if we keep living aesthetic it will never affect our beautiful supreme situation.

Our aesthetic situation is to be clean from the inside to the outside view of the world situation.

-First sport and healthy nutrition.
-Second, we dress in "Silk" while the d-evil was living in caves.
-Third, we Gentleman must become a sophisticated provider for the wife & child. *-I do not talk provider for the unaesthetic or for an Uncle Tom wife-.* The mother is the first teacher of a child and needs as a Lady of African Descent *(I do not talk unaesthetic woman)* special protection. We can´t bear to lose her during a car crash or by the hand of the **"BLUE - KLUX - KLAN"**. *- Cops Killing Blacks.* If we die we gonna leave everything on planet earth. We do not owe anything in this world, we just take care of our money & items.

If we Beautiful Brown Hu(e)man (hue = dark - man = race) Beings of African Descent understand that it is not necessary to support these racist fashion brands such as Chanel *(Jewish company, they consider "Blacks" as liquid money and played a major part in the "Black Slave Trade")*, racist Versace (they give "BLACKS" numbers, whenever we enter a Boutique, what means: Nigger we do not like you, but give us your "hard earned" money).

They do not even use "BLACK PEOPLE" as a marketing tool to get our money.

We Beautiful Brown Hu(e)man *(hue = dark - man = race)* Beings of the conscious Community *(not those 95er) (95% are Uncle Tom)* must understand the work of our own hand to support our Brothaz & Sistaz, that they can maintain their business. The end of their business is going to come immediately if we stop going to these fake Piggy Pink Brands.

Chapter 9

"Black America" have been begging all the presidents of the United States to come up with a master plan to save our African American Brothaz & Sistaz, that is the worst idea we ever had. If you begging these racist presidents, the only thing these "White presidents" are going to do is nothing more than "Cops Killing Blacks". More Racist Piggy Pink *(their history is written in blood all over the planet and stored in several archives around the globe)* who are trained to kill us. Why are we asking for that? You are not aware as a 95er *(95% are Uncle Toms)* of the fact that Piggy Pink divided us & created hate among ourselves = "Black on Black Crime". Are you conscious of the situation Brothaz & Sistaz, that there is a reason that mostly Gentleman of African Descent gets killed by the **"Blue - Klux - Klan?"** These presidents created that **"Black on Black Crime"**, that we have in these days. If we understand that Brothaz & Sistaz, you feel why it is important to form a unity and come together as one aesthetic empire to fix ourselves to force the d-evil for reparations.

The 1970's was the beginning in the USA of the gang war.

History of American ethnic crime:

You find that the Italians, the Irish &the European Jews lead the way when it comes to ethnic crime. The European Jew killed each other on the streets, the Irish killed each other in the streets, the Italians killed each other in the streets of America. They did not kill each other because they were born as criminals because they killed each other because America shut out these groups from realizing **the American Dream**.

Segregated to the poorest section in America. The Italians, the Irish, the European Jews, were not considered as "WHITE" human beings in America. They were poor none "White" trash. Poor none "White" trash was invented by the U.S Government. Why did the Government invent an entire system based on poor none "White" trash? The reason is that rich Piggy Pink *(their history is written in blood all over the planet and stored in several archives around the globe)* capitalism needed poor none "White" trash to build their corporate empires. If you start to study the great giants of financial capital, the Vanderbilt's (originally Dutch: Van der Bilt), the Rockefellers, the Morgans, you look @ any American leading families, you will find that many of them build their empires on the back of poor people. The only way they were able to build their empire on the backs of poor people, is by keeping a large segment of the American citizen of none "White" people poor & homeless.

Our Brothaz and Sistaz must understand, that capitalism can not survive without a very big source of cheap labour. Before Slavery poor none "White" trash *(European Jews, Italians, Irish)* were the source of capital.

In 1619 the enslaving of People of African Descent, we were not considered to be people. We were "Black" items, merchandise, products to trade with.

The lowest of the low in the social hierarchy in America, was the so-called European Jew, Irish and Italian people. They were the last valued people in the American social order. They were socially down @ the bottom. And we people of African Descent were seen as items. We were not seen as living hu*(e)*man *(hue = dark - man = race)* beings from Africa. America was built on the first level on poor none "White" trash. - you need to understand, they were not given jobs, health care, education. Guess what: They fought each other in the streets, they got drunk *(alcoholic)*, they would beat their women and they started gangs. One of the reasons the American Government started to intervene on "White on White Crime" is because it began to drive population numbers down. In other words, if we let Piggy Pink People kill Piggy Pink *(their history is written in blood all over the planet and stored in several archives around the globe)* we are going to lose our numbers in this country. Piggy Pink *(their history is written in blood all over the planet and stored in several archives around the globe)* needed unity to keep African Americans & Native Americans down. They needed Piggy Pink People *(their history is written in blood all over the planet and stored in several archives around the globe)* for World war 1 & 2. America needed to come up with a plan to stop "White on White Crime"

Let's face the situation from the psychological perspective. Why were so many Piggy Pink People *(their history is written in blood all over the planet and stored in several archives around the globe)* killed? Because of unemployment, it causes depression. Not being able to provide for your family it causes depression that leads to alcoholism, it triggers domestic abuse, low self-esteem. It engenders a certain kind of anger and disappointment. Piggy Pink *(their history is written in blood all over the planet and stored in several archives around the globe)* killed each other, for the same reasons African Descent People killed each other. That was because they were angry @ the fact they were not allowed to lead a proper life.

We take the movie **"GANGS OF NEW YORK"** as an example, it is an excellent film that shows how Piggy Pink *(their history is written in blood all over the planet and stored in several archives around the globe)* gangs did everything, what African Americans do today. Piggy Pink People *(their history is written in blood all over the planet and stored in several archives around the globe)* were the original drug dealers & killers. **But in 1940 America decided that they gonna upgrade, the European Jew, the Irish people, the Italian people to Piggy**

Pink (their history is written in blood all over the planet and stored in several archives around the globe) **status**. Before the year 1940 if you were Irish, a so-called European Jew or Italian, you were not seen as part of the "White Race". They started to give them officially financial support by loaning money to these groups that they could get out of the ghetto.

It went then from "White on White" Crime to Piggy Pink (their history is written in blood all over the planet and stored in several archives around the globe) on African American crime, but of course, they do not talk about that. Why do they never talk about, how the Irish use to hang the "Black" people? Why do they hate to talk about, how the Piggy Pink Race *(their history is written in blood all over the planet and stored in several archives around the globe)* use to hang "Black" people in the 20th, 30th, 40th and 50th? Why do they do not like to talk about it, how the European Jews used to beat us up and hang African Americans?
"Black on Black Crime" did not really existed until the 1960's, because we were segregated and was forced to do on our own. We had jobs, we had "Black Wall-street", it was until 1968 when the United States killed Dr. Martin Luther King. They went to the inner city and deindustrialized the inner African American structure. They shut down the factories, they shut down the industrial trade train programmes

We were plumbers, we were electricians, we were carpenters, we were barbers, we were woodworkers, we were stone masons, we were auto-mechanics, we were auto body repairs, we were seamen, ...African Americans had over 50 trades that we were able to use to feed our families. There was no gang banging yet. We African Americans did not start gangs yet until the majority lost their jobs. "Blacks" had not the time to be in a gang, back in those days until they got tricked to lose their jobs. So the gangs began to resolve as a reaction of not being able to provide for our families, it was an economic castration by Piggy Pink People (their history is written in blood all over the planet and stored in several archives around the globe) of the United States of America. These gangs evolved as an economic reaction to Piggy Pink People (their history is written in blood all over the planet and stored in several archives around the globe) America financial castration of the African American male. There would be no damn gangs if they did not start financially castrating people of African Descent because if we had jobs, we did not have time for gangs.

The only person who can really be part of a gang is an unemployed African-American. I gonna take it a step further! The primary "JOB OF A GANG" the primary "FUNCTION OF A GANG" is not violence it is to give their members a certain kind of employment to make money. Legal or illegal. Selling Drugs, prostitution, hustle credit cards, running numbers. The "GANG" is a labour union. So from a certain perspective, the United States Government is responsible for "BLACK GANGS"- ever been created. Because if you never created the economic destitution that is gripping the African-American Community, there would have never been a need for "GANGS". What we need to do is to stop asking these Piggy Pink Racist *(their history is written in blood all over the planet and stored in several archives around the globe)* presidents of the United States to solve our problems. If we force any Piggy Pink (their history is written in blood all over the planet and stored in several archives around the globe), president of the United States, to bring in the Army, the **"Blue - Klux - Klan"** to help us, I am telling you the only thing we gonna have to happen is trained **"Cops Killing Black"**. We gonna have more Trayvon Martins, we gonna have more Alton Sterlings, we gonna have more Philando Catilles, we gonna have more Korryn Gaines ... the only thing that is going to happen, if we keep on begging these racist Piggy Pink *(their history is written in blood all over the planet and stored in several archives around the globe)* presidents of the United States, we gonna get more Piggy Pink *(their history is written in blood all over the planet and stored in several archives around the globe)* extermination of African Americans. We must finally understand Piggy Pink People presidents of the United States! Piggy Pink *(their history is written in blood all over the planet and stored in several archives around the globe)* do not like us. They have never been our friends and they never plan to see us equal as them. -If you are a part of the Uncle Tom problem in our African Descent Community and do not confirm these facts, please put my book away immediately.

Why are you asking them to solve your African-American Problems?
The Mother of all violence is mis-education.
The father of all violence is economical castration.

Half of the African Americans Men in America are unemployed in percentage terms 75% are without a job.

The Piggy Pink labour union in every city does systematically keep the percentage of African-American Men to get trained to be skilled to become labors on a minimum low, and then they hire Piggy Pink Presidents of the United States, we gonna get more Piggy Pink *(their history is written in blood all over the planet and stored in several archives around the globe)* boys in maximum numbers, with African Americans tax dollars. I set the record straight about that sort of racism in the labor unions, with which the Piggy Pink Presidents of the United States, we gonna get more Piggy Pink (their history is written in blood all over the planet and stored in several archives around the globe) Government who is complicit by making these unions.

We do not need more from the **"Blue - Klux - Klan"** to solve our problems.

Chapter 10

Piggy Pink Supremacy *(their history is written in blood all over the planet and stored in several archives around the globe)* /
formerly known as "White Supremacy is based upon the pseudo-science of "racial realism" also known as scientific racism.
Scientific racist cite iQ studies as the foundation of their fundamentalist belief system that Piggy Pink People *(their history is written in blood all over the planet and stored in several archives around the globe)* are better and superior to Beautiful Brown Hu*(e)*man *(hue = dark - man = race)* Beings. The fundamentalism of these Piggy Pink Supremacists *(their history is written in blood all over the planet and stored in several archives around the globe)* is based upon the thoroughly debunked "research" Neo-Nazi Hitler sympathizing institution like the mankind quarterly & the Pioneer Fund, Ku Klux Klansman like Ernest S. Cox, and racial sterilization advocates like Richard Lynn.

In the Piggy Pink People Supremacy/ formerly known as White Supremacy *(their history is written in blood all over the planet and stored in several archives around the globe)* pamphlet "Bell Curve" the main claim regarding a low African iQ in relation to Europeans comes from a 1989 apartheid-era South African Junior Aptitude test, that was administered to 1,000 16-year-old African students who did not speak English as a native language. They scored a mean of 69 on the test and Piggy Pink Supremacist *(their history is written in blood all over the planet and stored in several archives around the globe)* Richard Lynn extrapolated this mean iQ onto an entire continent of Africa.

These two Piggy Pink surveys *(their history is written in blood all over the planet and stored in several archives around the globe)* completely eviscerate the belief system of these Piggy Pink Racist *(their history is written in blood all over the planet and stored in several archives around the globe)*.

These d-evilish Piggy Pink People *(their history is written in blood all over the planet and stored in several archives around the globe)* is to be seen as the character in the classical novel: **THE EMPERORS NEW CLOTHES!** 95% confirm he has special clothes on, except those 2 tailors and a child who is telling the truth by screaming:**"But there is nothing special, he is just naked!"**

We take that fictional novel character as our guide, these Piggy Pink People *(their history is written in blood all over the planet and stored in several archives around the globe)* methods, always alter their belief system, when they get a sunburn by the light of truth.

At the beginning of the 20th century, Piggy Pink Supremacy *(their history is written in blood all over the planet and stored in several archives around the globe)* were saying that the tendency for "Blacks" to do far better on memory skill tests than "Whites" was due to their being "closer to the primitive state" where memory was more important and functional than higher order skills, logic, reasons, etc.! Then 10 years later, when testing began to show that the children of rich Piggy Pink People *(their history is written in blood all over the planet and stored in several archives around the globe)* scored better on memory tests, these same Piggy Pink Supremacists once again changed their minds when new memory tests showed that poor and kids from African Descent with low iQ's had excellent memories that surpassed those of wealthier folks and Piggy Pinks *(their history is written in blood all over the planet and stored in several archives around the globe)*.

The same shifting arguments have occurred with regard to the test of "reaction time." -when tests have demonstrated that people of African Descent have the quicker reaction time to various external stimuli, Piggy Pink

Supremacist (their history is written in blood all over the planet and stored in several archives around the globe) take this as proof that they were intellectually and emotionally inferior, less reflective and analytic. But when some test have demonstrated a Piggy Pink *(their history is written in blood all over the planet and stored in several archives around the globe)* edge on reaction time, these same Piggy Pink Supremacist *(their history is written in blood all over the planet and stored in several archives around the globe)* have claimed, it was a sign of having "quicker brains." Similarly, throughout the years, Piggy Pink Supremacist have claimed that "Blacks" evolved later, and are thus inferior.

Chapter 11

By trying to integrate into the Piggy Pink Society *(their history is written in blood all over the planet and stored in several archives around the globe)* We Africans have integrated ourselves into nothingness. No inner stability, unemployment *(75% have no jobs and live on welfare)*. No, inner values, no nationalism like the Asians, the Arabs, the Turks, the French! No, identity of ourselves because we try to become a copy of Piggy Pink People *(their history is written in blood all over the planet and stored in several archives around the globe)*. In these days Africans referred even the word N!gger to themselves that has been designed by our slave masters, the evilest word created by the devil to let us feel, less than a hu*(e)*man *(hue = dark . man = race)*. Africans silently agree to Piggy Pink unwritten *(their history is written in blood all over the planet and stored in several archives around the globe)* rules, so that they can live under the illusion of inclusion in the Piggy Pink *(their history is written in blood all over the planet and stored in several archives around the globe)* environment, without being aware what devilish situation they are in - 95er *(95 % are Uncle Toms)*.

Author of this book:

Say the N-Word to me as a Piggy Pink "Man" I request you then to be a "Man" and ran faster than me because I have 0% Uncle Tom DNA in my body, you going to have a big problem. -Physically!

I gonna turn from a British African Descent Gentleman into an African-American thug and make your life a living hell.

How did I escape Piggy Pink Supremacy?

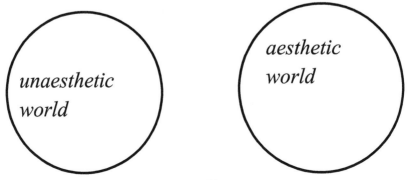

Aesthetic vs. the unaesthetic

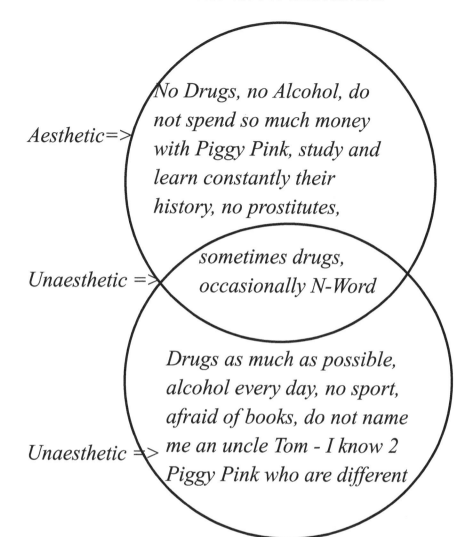

Aesthetic=>
No Drugs, no Alcohol, do not spend so much money with Piggy Pink, study and learn constantly their history, no prostitutes,

Unaesthetic =>
sometimes drugs, occasionally N-Word

Unaesthetic =>
Drugs as much as possible, alcohol every day, no sport, afraid of books, do not name me an uncle Tom - I know 2 Piggy Pink who are different

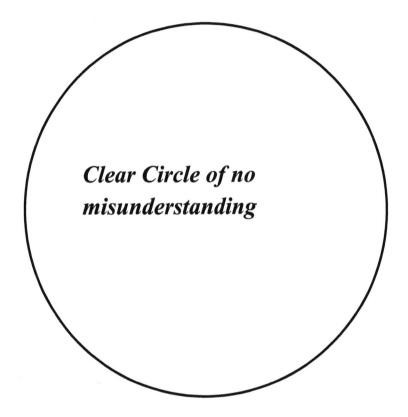

Clear Circle of no misunderstanding

A gambling situation. A bubble full of illusions. What happens if you gamble and keep gambling? The Bubble is going to burst one day. All you gonna have as an end result is something strange unaesthetic.= welcome to the destiny of an Uncle Tom

So, why shall I as an aesthetic individual waste my time in an unaesthetic bubble that is going to blow up one day?
Walk away from the unaesthetic even if it requires to walk through life without a loving partner on your side.

A King can only be in unity with a Queen.
A Gentleman can only be with a Lady, - not girly trash
An aesthetic individual can only live in harmony with someone who speaks the same language.

Walk away from all sorts of none sense, from all these looser, who leads an unaesthetic existence, from a long-term perspective. Your life is valuable and needs to be protected.

There are not many people I can really vibe with. I could've vibe with Malcolm X and the late Dr. Martin Luther King (not the - I have a dream - preacher). I can vibe with my Brotha David Banner, he truly does these Afro-Centric things, that is going to form younger generations.

Chapter 12

Let me tell you why we have Uncle Toms, Thugz and so many differences in our African Descent Community: Some of us are individuals - the majority - and some of us are Nationalist or Afro-Centrics. We Afro-Centrics view the world, what is in the very best interest of our African Descent Community to take power away from Piggy Pink *(their history is written in blood all over the planet and stored in several archives around the globe)* People/Racism. I wanna be clear about it, there is no middle way. You either go for all those unwritten rules created by the racist dominant society or you separate yourself as much as you can from the Piggy Pink Racist Society *(their history is written in blood all over the planet and stored in several archives around the globe)* - Everybody has to make that decision only by himself. Am I gonna be for my African Descent people or am I gonna join the game created by the d-evil.

One of the reason why Beautiful Brown Hu*(e)*man (hue = dark - man = race) Beings are in a situation, where we are in right now, is simply the fact that most of us conform to Piggy Pink People *(their history is written in blood all over the planet and stored in several archives around the globe)* unwritten rules.

Now, let's compare Uncle Tom people mindset to the Jewish community: They *(Jews)* operate as a collective union. A Jew can only be born of a Jewish mother. It means the future wife must convert to Judaism. When it comes to Jewish imperialism and control, they put their differences to the side and create a nationalist agenda: What is in the best interest of all in the Jewish community? The same with Europeans/the Piggy Pink race/- ist. When it comes, how to keep the **"BLACKS"** under control, they come together under one roof to discuss a strategy. The Arabs have exactly the same pattern. The group and the belief system comes first. How do they deal in China, when they catch you working against the will of the group? You might get killed.

I gonna give you the biggest reason why we are where we are. We can not send our children to the same school system, who enslaved our ancestors, thinking they gonna somehow solve the problem, that they cause. Our oppressors will never teach our children, how to free yourself in this oppression. His job is to keep you under control of the Piggy Pink racist system. I can prove it to you: "Slavery ended in America 1865. Where is our big time "BLACK" fortune 500 company? Where are our "BLACK OWN" fortune 500 supermarkets? Where are our "BLACK" distribution networks? Where are our publicly traded companies on wall-street? Where are our independent schools? Where are our Haute Couture Brands? How do you explain that to me? Except you hate your African Descent root and willing to accept those racist people for little money."

The whole system by the Piggy Pink Race/-ist Society (*their history is written in blood all over the planet and stored in several archives around the globe*) has been designed to let us fail. Everybody comes to America to own something. Asians come to America to sell wigs and weaves to stupid dump "Blacks," (*because Piggy Pink told these women, we are going to accept you "if you walk around with a smelly wig/weaves*). The Asians come basically to build up a "China-Town", it means we African

Americans are not allowed to set up a business in their "China Town", but we are welcome to bring & spend our money in "China Town." (Do Asians see "BLACKS AS LIQUID MONEY," TOO)?
Russians come to America - in general to the western European world - to owe something. In Berlin there is a district called Charlotten-Grad (Stalingrad), it is a diaspora only for Russian migrants. Even if you need a funeral ceremony you go to a Russian provider.

Chapter 13

You can't have sex with Piggy Pink *(their history is written in blood all over the planet and stored in several archives around the globe)* and talk "Black"
you are automatically an Uncle Tom, who can't be taken seriously in our Aesthetic world of Beautiful Brown Human Beings because you must obey to his/her Piggy Pink Supremacy standard of racism *(their history is written in blood all over the planet and stored in several archives around the globe)*. He/She from the Piggy Pink race can never relate to our struggle nor is interested to stop racism or would devote his/her time to destroy Piggy Pink supremacy.

I wanna make that clear, if you have that Donald Sterling Sugar Daddy syndrome, sex in exchange for money, sex in exchange for a car, sex in exchange for Jewish racist products, such as a Chanel bag, sex in exchange to live under the illusion of inclusion in an unaesthetic bubble that equals a gambling situation, it means it is predictable when the bubble is about to burst. Please, do not put the guilt on the "Master!"

According to Donald Sterling *(a billionaire who hates "Blacks!" He was the owner of the NBA basketball Team - L.A Clippers and placed his Piggy Pink dick between those legs of a Sugar Baby of African Descent)* **"Blacks"** are no longer needed in the United States, they were only brought here to do labour for free. Furthermore, he explained we gave them something to eat, a place to sleep. And now they complain and started killing each other.

Racist Sugar Daddy Donald Sterling shows every aspect of a slave master. He made money as a real estate developer, back in those days. This Jewish *(Jews consider Blacks are liquid money)* hypocrite could not be found guilty as a racist immediately, but everybody knew silently that he had that slave master mentality. This devilish, fucking Piggy Pink-Cracker *(their history is written in blood all over the planet and stored in several archives around the globe)* gave everything a clear face of no misunderstanding. You need to understand, he is not a truck driver, he is not an uneducated "working Class" racist from a Piggy Pink *(oink, oink) (their history is written in blood all over the planet and stored in several archives around the globe)* trailer park, he is financially independent enough to place his dick exclusively in a Piggy Pink *(their history is written in blood all over the planet and stored in several archives around the globe)* racist young Piggy Pink Russian pin-up beauty. How to pretend not to be a racist? Very simple: Hide yourself all the time among people of African Descent-like the racist singer Justin Bieber ***(a so-called joke by the singer: Why is a "Black" afraid of a chainsaw? Answer: RNNNN...NIGGA-NIGGA-NIGGA)***! - engine sound of that tool.

These wicked, racist, Piggy Pink People *(their history is written in blood all over the planet and stored in several archives around the globe)* will always find a 95er *(95% are uncle Toms)* to hide the true racist identity.

Chapter 14

Make Beautiful Brown Hu*(e)*man *(hue = dark - man = race)* Beings of African Descent think, their problem is not the Piggy Pink *(oink, oink)* Racist society *(their history is written in blood all over the planet and stored in several archives around the globe),* they make you believe it is your own dilemma, that you failed as an individual.

These talented "Pimps" mainly athletes, entertainers, speaks only to the middle class. The real DNA rich do not behave in a new money way, like these unsophisticated African Americans. The poor can only sit in front of a TV to watch MTV-Cribs, the middle class is not a part of the -**By DNA-Rich World**.

And these so-called "Rappers, Sports celebrities" like Mike Tyson end up all the time financially broke. After they have brought their income back into the racist system *(Prada, Versace, racist Chanel...)* of Piggy Pink People *(their history is written in blood all over the planet and stored in several archives around the globe)* they do not owe almost any valuable wealth, not-refundable expansive brands, created by Piggy Pink *(their history is written in blood all over the planet and stored in several archives around the globe)* designers and manufactured in Asia. The Average African American Athletes puts his money into clothing, cars and expansive Piggy Pink *(their history is written in blood all over the planet and stored in several archives around the globe)* Russian pin-up beauties *(Russian Woman: "Actually, these Niggers are not my type, but if they are willing to put money on the table...")*!

I remember returning home 3 months ago, I started my computer to see a documentary by the name: BROKE. It was only about African American celebrities, who have gone bankrupt. And some of the names on the list blew my mind because I did not know that they were broke. The list contained about 500 different African American Celebrities from the Hollywood movie world, music world & sports world. Who was new money rich - not DNA Rich.

Chapter 15

Why African Descent Unity & How? The answer is very simple: Unify!

What does unity look like, why should we really unify? The way to solve major problems is to work backwards to identify the root of the problem. Why does it exist? Our African Descent problem is our oppression. That we are allowed to be mistreated on a global level by all these unhealthy looking Piggy Pink *(oink, oink) People (their history is written in blood all over the planet and stored in several archives around the globe)* and additionally by Asians, Russians, Arabs. We are the least respected group on the planet, wherever we go.

We take the African Americans as our guide example: They allow themselves to be mistreated by Asians, by Indians, by Arabs and of course by the number one enemy the so-called "White Race "with a Piggy Pink skin complexion. Why are we still mistreated like we are not valuable, Beautiful Brown Hu(e)man *(hue = dark - man = race)* Beings? Because the infrastructure in the United States was created by averaging the labour and averaging the hu(e)man *(hue = dark - man = race)* labour of Africans as capital. The system itself was created by African slaves in mind, in sense to make America great on the backs of Africans. America, especially the south, was only built with&on Africans, who had to work for free.

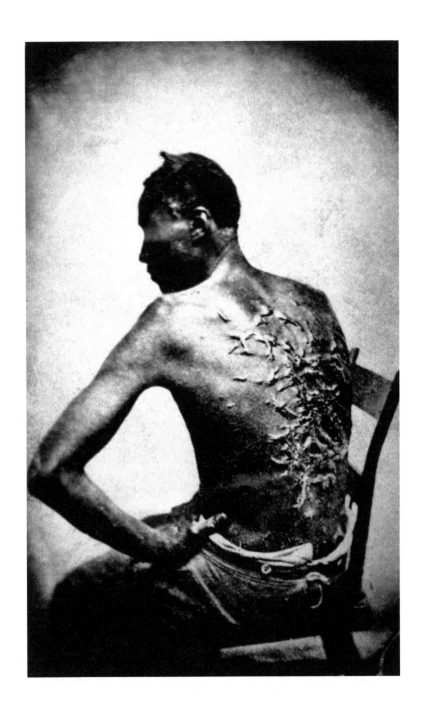

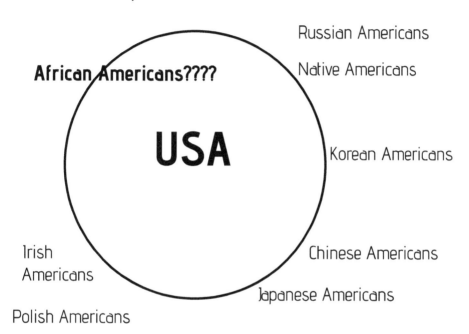

Portuguese Americans

Russian Americans

Native Americans

African Americans????

USA

Korean Americans

Irish
Americans

Chinese Americans

Japanese Americans

Polish Americans

All these American Subcultures have their luxury to be in America to work on their American Dream.

- But we African Americans had been made to live in America and we are the only group, they can not get rid off by sending them home. Piggy Pink *(their history is written in blood all over the planet and stored in several archives around the globe)* **brought us over against our will.**

All these other American subcultures have many things in common, what we Africans do not have ...

- Therefore African Americans are allowed to be treated differently than anyone else.

During World War 2, Japanese Americans were put into a separate area, because, Piggy Pink (their history is written in blood all over the planet and stored in several archives around the globe) were afraid they gonna revolt against the Government. So they locked them up in camps for 2 years. So, America had to pay reparations to the ancestors of the descendants of Japanese Americans. For those 2 years of locked up in a separate area. America was held accountable by the **World Core** to give reparations.
All countries Russia, Korea, China, Japan, Poland, Portugal...etc... have a homeland, where America is responsible for their national origins and America has a responsibility to the **World Core.** All these countries are a part of the **World Core**. America has to answer to the **World Core** for each single country.
For African-Americans, there is no direct homeland or

nation or nationality to support African Americans.

So, America does not have to be held accountable for human rights violations against African Americans. Because there is nobody to fight for them. <u>So, if we stand up for ourselves we are considered radical.</u> All we are taught to do is:

Play 95er (95% are Uncle Tom) and take the pain.

Uncle Tom: "If someone slaps your face turn the other cheek. They do not mean it; not every Piggy Pink is a devil, I know three who are fine...!"

Remember the United States was founded on a revolution. Great Britain is the "Old Sophisticated Mother" with very old-fashioned traditions. America, she is the younger vulgar daughter, who has not grown up yet. America is still a developing country. Americans celebrate the July 4th because America wanted to have autonomy and King George of England wouldn't allow the United States to be an Independent union.

But America still forbids to revolt for our rights, Piggy Pink *(their history is written in blood all over the planet and stored in several archives around the globe)* is telling the World Core: "We are radicals."

<u>Let's break this down:</u> We are not unified and there is no country in the world that backs us up. This is why African Americans are held powerless and allowed to be oppressed. There are several injustices, killings, mass incarceration, the war on drugs, gang violence. All these things that are happened under the leadership of the Christianity supported by the American Government, there is nobody from the "World Core" to back us up. The Continent of Africa can't back us because it has multiple countries.

In order to liberate ourselves to become an empire of deep aesthetic Beautiful Brown Hu(e)man (hue = dark - man = race) Beings, how to fix this problem?

African Americans vs. Every other subculture

- We have no identity *(like all these other subcultures)*
- We have no flag
- We have no home country *(Land)*
- We have no consistent culture *(even Native Americans have a consistent culture)*
- We have no National Anthem

Kingdom of Aesthetic for Beautiful Brown Hu*(e)*man *(hue = dark - man = race)* Beings of African Descent: Until we unify, we can't make any demand.

No unity, the result is:

- Lack of Self-pride *(too many of those "WHITE WASHED" Uncle Toms)*

- Lack of Self-worth (too many of those "WHITE WASHED" Uncle Toms)

- Lack of dignity

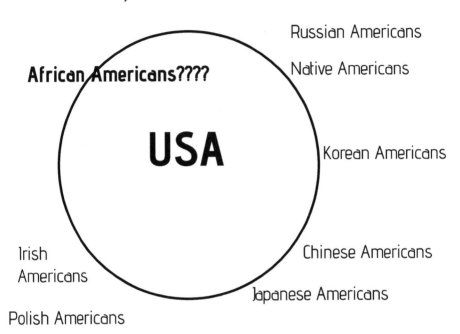

- Lack of Unity
- Lack of culture
- LACK OF POWER!!! - There is nothing bigger in ourselves, then being a 95er (95% are Uncle Toms)! There is nothing in ourselves then to accept their Piggy Pink "God" (their history is written in blood all over the planet and stored in several archives around the globe).

We were kidnapped and brought to America, for only one reason: To serve as properties for the d-d-evilish unhealthy looking (oink-oink), Piggy Pink conqueror *(their history is written in blood all over the planet and stored in several archives around the globe).*
We were lynched in America, we have been mas incarcerated in America, we were Jim Crowed in America, we were drugged in America, we have been hated ever since in America, we have never been seen as Beautiful Brown Hu*(e)*man *(hue = dark - man = race)* Beings in America, we have never received justice in America, we have never received reparations by the United States of America, we are still getting killed by the cops *(Blue - Klux - Klan),* We have been brutalized in America, we have been unequaled school systemed here.

But we have one thing in common: It is - us - Beautiful Brown Hu*(e)*man Beings *(hue = dark - man = race)*. It is our pain&our trauma. It means we have to unify, that pain, that trauma under one flag of the Kingdom of Aesthetic. Right now, America is our home country, we got to be a Beautiful Brown Hu*(e)*man Being *(hue = dark - man = race)* nation under the flag of the Kingdom of Aesthetic.

Self Imposed Vote:

If we take our top 51 African Descent influencer I do not mean Uncle Toms or 101 influencers of African Descent who are not scared to step out of the circle of those 95er.

We do VOTE for one common name for our true Aesthetic identity, how we wanna name ourselves:

African Americans, Pan Africans, New Africans, United Africans of America, United Africans and America.

BROWN PEOPLE OF AFRICAN DESCENT, BROWN HUMAN BEINGS OF AFRICAN DESCENT, BROWN PEOPLE,

We VOTE for our own chosen identity! 51 or 101 of our top influencer - Example: Mr. X & Mr. Y ...
MR. X is going to get elected by the majority of our brothaz, he is then our so-called delegate, who is in charge to choose a name, where we can say, we are proud of that label. And we decided for ourselves, not the Piggy Pink Race. And that would be our true nationality and nobody can take it away from us. We gonna then make Aesthetic history because we do for "Ourselves." Stop let anybody else control us.

We need to become one nation of Brown Hu*(e)*man *(hue = dark - man = race)* Beings in the nation of America, in the European nation and worldwide.

We need to unify under one aesthetic colour given by ourselves, what is our beautiful Brown Human Beings - dark brown, brown or light brown skin complexion and not as "BLACK - Merchandise, properties, products, n!ggaz.

We need to unify under one aesthetic "Self" identity that is our, pain&trauma, post-slavery syndrome.

We need to identify under one aesthetic "Self" identity to fix ourselves, our household, our family situation, that we Beautiful Brown Hu*(e)*man *(hue = dark - man = race)* Beings of the Kingdom of Aesthetic can force the devil to give us reparations. We want 10 - 12 States in America, govern and controlled by an AFRICAN-AMERICAN UNITY = KINGDOM OF AESTHETIC

How to do it?

Well, "Self-Imposed Vote" only for African Americans or People of African Descent. If someone has the right to put a name or a label on you ("BLACK"), you do not have power. We were captured/ kidnapped by Piggy Pink *(their history is written in blood all over the planet and stored in several archives around the globe)*, however, no Piggy Pink is allowed to give his vote.

As a unified Beautiful Brown Hu*(e)*man *(hue = dark - man = race)* Being nation, here is what might happen: The "World Core" law says that a nation can be established, we can establish our own legal aesthetic nation of Beautiful Brown Hu*(e)*man *(hue = dark - man = race)* Beings. Not a fake nationality is given by Piggy Pink racist people. Right now, we have no acceptance nor support by the "World Core." But if a critical mass of people *(51 & 101)* acknowledge themselves as:

African Americans, Pan Africans, New Africans, United Africans of America, United Africans and America.

BROWN PEOPLE OF AFRICAN DESCENT, BROWN HUMAN BEINGS OF AFRICAN DESCENT, BROWN PEOPLE,
and self-determine enough, civilized, sophisticated enough to acknowledge themselves as an Aesthetic Hu*(e)*man *(hue = dark - man = race)* Being, with equal rights, we can win the fight against Piggy Pink *(their history is written in blood all over the planet and stored in several archives around the globe)* . Because we are organized then and force the d-evil without these Uncle Toms to give us reparations. We gonna bring our case of African Descent holocaust to the "World Core."- And the Piggy Pink d-evil owes us a lot. But first, we need to fix our problems within the aesthetic nation for ourselves to acknowledge ourselves. Then, we can force America and the rest of the Piggy Pink *(their history is written in blood all over the planet and stored in several archives around the globe)* world to stop with the racist bullshit.
That is how to get power to be organized and acknowledge ourselves. We gonna have our own bank holidays, our own National Anthem, maybe written by Alica Keys, our own flag, - ain't nobody stopin' but us from doin' this! - you feelin' me?

Message to Uncle Toms: It is o.k. to be independent. I do not say kill your Piggy Pink wife or husband. We were great aesthetic human beings of African Descent before. I say let's build something up on our own by unification. We none Uncle Toms wanna identify ourselves with our aesthetic soul and spirit. As an African born in the Caribbean, it is a must for me to stand up. I just proved to you we are not seen as equals, we are the most oppressed hu(e)man (hue = dark - man = race) kind in the world to all the other nationalities because we do not have what they have.

So Mr.&Mrs. Uncle Tom, in order to be equal, we need to give to ourselves, what every other subculture got, what we do not have. It is not in my interest to divide you from a Piggy Wife or Piggy Pink husband. If you consider remaining in that fantasy bubble for the sake of your "relationship" so pray to the real lord.

Chapter 16

Is this book of Aesthetic for Beautiful Brown Hu(e)man *(hue = dark - man = race)* Beings, the brand to stop racism against the first hu*(e)*man race on planet earth a rage of violence? Let's break the word **-rage-** down. According to the dictionary: **Rage = fury, violent, venom, violent speak, rage - uncontrolled anger**, is this the language of an aesthetic hu*(e)*man being? How then - I address this message to the so-called better race, who label themselves as "White," who are so more sophisticated than me as a **"BLACK"**-

Is your footprints in the world history written in blood or our African Descent story. Explain it to me, if I am so full of negativity&hate that my words transformed hu*(e)*man *(hue = dark - man = race)* life to become wiser and conscious. The words I speak goes into the traumatized psyche of a Beautiful Brown Hu*(e)*man *(hue = dark - man = race)* woman of African descent.....

According to a Sista from London: "Thank you very much brotha, you opened my eyes. Once I used to hate my brown skin, once I refused to date "BLACK" - now I see Beauty in our Beautiful Brown Hu*(e)*man *(hue = dark - man = race)* Being Race. Because, if I fall for a Piggy Pink, it means I hate the skin complexion of my mother from African Descent."

According to a brother who goes by the name O.J.and is 13 years younger my age:"You speak all the time the god damn truth. You know how things work because of you I consider to attend evening school and stop drinking alcohol during the morning time." Well, Mr. Piggy Pink, I am not an individual of rage, all I do is to speak the truth, based on one very simple clear fact: *Your history is written in blood all over the planet.*

Those words of truth it touches the soul of my brothaz & sistaz. They used to be lost like myself in those days until they discovered what it needs to decode your Piggy Pink Supremacy. They changed the way they live, they started to do sport, they started to question your wicked racist Piggy Pink *(their history is written in blood all over the planet and stored in several archives around the globe)* system. They decided like brotha Malcolm X to turn their life from sitting in front of a TV to read and study to become a part of our aesthetic future Kingdom. This is truly not a book of rage, this is all factz Mr. Racist - D-evil - Piggy Pink *(their history is written in blood all over the planet and stored in several archives around the globe)*.

What is it that makes my brothaz and sistaz turn to their own roots of African Descent, after they spoke to me, after they spend few hours with me, after they entered my house, ...

According to another former friend, what is it that a friend told me about a common good friend:
"...Alexander, talks about you, like as if he was in a candy store?" What is it that makes people turn around when I enter a restaurant and try to get in touch with me? What is it that causes the change from a "BLACK" - from a "Thug" who hear my words? It is a common spirit of deep inner aesthetic.

Piggy Pink *(oink-oink)***"God!"** We were on the planet before your *(oink-oink)* Piggy Pink Race and your so-called **"God!"** Why don't you teach the truth about your wicked, hypocritical, unhealthy looking, fucking, devilish, racist, humankind? Why don't you teach our African Descent Community, that you have been around only for 6000 years of time and we as the very first race of Beautiful Brown Hu*(e)*man *(hue = dark - man = race)* Beings for 66 trillions of years?

My book is not for you Piggy Pink *(their history is written in blood all over the planet and stored in several archives around the globe)*, not for those 95er *(95% are Uncle Tom)*, it is for people who are @ a crossroad of their life and need a guide through your Piggy Pink *(their history is written in blood all over the planet and stored in several archives around the globe)*, wicked racist world to raise them as what they really are: **Beautiful Brown Hu*(e)*man** *(hue = dark . man = race)* **Beings of African Descent, with a deeper touch to something bigger in the universe.** - Have you ever teach that to my brothaz and sistaz? A question to you 95er *(95% are Uncle Tom)*: "Has your Piggy Pink racist fucker ever told you that? Why doesn't he/she tells the truth, if they are from the sophisticated better, finer race?

But since I had looked @ the word: **Rage**...! I went to open another dictionary. **Rage** could also mean:

something popular, something "En Vogue," something that is elegant, something that is fancy, the hot spot, the last word, the latest "Thing," = the "iN - Thing." Is that what gets you in "rage" Mr. Racist, when it comes to our Aesthetic African Descent Hu*(e)*man (hue = dark - man = race) Being race? -? - ? Because our African Hu*(e)*man *(hue= dark - man = race)* kind is the ***"Rage of the world"*** *(Michael Jackson, Michael Air Jordan, Serena Williams, Tiger Woods, Magic Johnson, Beyoncé, Rhianna, Oprah Winfrey, Puff Daddy, Will Smith, Singer Prince ...etc.)*!

You are afraid to lose power that should deceive and oppress your former slaves of African Descent. But Piggy Pink *(their history is written in blood all over the planet and stored in several archives around the globe)* can´t tell the truth.

According to a newspaper in Piggy Pink United States *(their history is written in blood all over the planet and stored in several archives around the globe)*:

We are Americans whose diversity, faith and race unite us against bigotry.

Allow me to ask you Piggy Pink guys: "When and where in the United States of Piggy Pink America did that happen?"

We are Americans who know the rights and dignity in all of us are jeopardized when those any of us are challenged.

Allow me to ask you Piggy Pink guys: "When did you come to that level of consciousness?"

All these devilish words sound so nice. You came to Africa so nice, we trusted you and now you try to seduce us again so nice.

Still according to a newspaper in Piggy Pink *(oink -oink)* United States:
We are Americans, who reject the ugly slender of behaviour among us seeking to lift up some Americans by revelling others.
Allow me to ask you Piggy Pink guys: Is that how you got to be "White Supremacist? Lifting up yourself and revelling all other dark people on the earth?"

Let me break that, not new hypocritical Piggy Pink *(their history is written in blood all over the planet and stored in several archives around the globe)* statement down.

Well, we from the Aesthetic nation see ourselves as the first-born race on the planet- **factz, factz, factz**. There has no been no other born as the first hu*(e)*man *(hue = dark - man = race)* on planet earth, then Beautiful Brown Hu*(e)*man Beings. -**Factz, factz, factz**. There has nobody been born on the planet who has a devil attitude like your "human" kind. By the way, we do not see you as a "human"
There has nobody been born from your race, that we consider being friends - only these 95er *(95% are Uncle Toms)* and

if any Piggy Pink *(their history is written in blood all over the planet and stored in several archives around the globe)* feels verbally attacked by this book; well I gonna break even that down: "How many years have these so-called "WHITES" been verbally and physically and still attacking Beautiful Brown Hu*(e)*man *(hue = dark - man = race)* Beings of African Descent with a deeper aesthetic spirit?

Does it mean -Piggy Pink *(their history is written in blood all over the planet and stored in several archives around the globe)* - you can´t take what you still dish out and still doing to us??? - **you fucking racist, you fucking cracker, you fucking d-evil, you one kind evil creature son of a bitch!** - *Racism does not deserve to be named differently.* The day of deceiving Beautiful Brown Hu*(e)*man *(hue = dark - man = race)* Beings of African Descent is forever over.

Chapter 17

Aesthetic - The Brand to stop racism against our BROTHAZ&SISTAZ of AFRICAN DESCENT. We must learn to understand the condition we are in. If we live and grow up as Beautiful Brown Hu*(e)*man *(hue = dark - man = race)* Beings in a certain unaesthetic, not the inspirational environment, we must become what we are today. Post-slavery traumatized Beautiful Brown Hu*(e)*man *(hue = dark - man = race)* Beings, destroyed from the inside, who gonna run for the big goal to be accepted by the d-d-d-evilish Piggy Pink (their history is written in blood all over the planet and stored in several archives around the globe) race. These "White Washed" Uncle Toms *(95% are Uncle Toms)* try so hard that they even risk losing their hair from all these treatments. Whatever environment we are in, we become an extension of that. If you hang out with unaesthetic people you learn to speak their slang. If you deal with these low self-esteem small size millionaire you stay on that level of dept and loans. If you waste your time only with aesthetic things that are bigger than any humankind you find the true "Lord" within yourself.

You gonna Succeed in becoming something unexplained bigger in life, then these Piggy Pink People can never achieve. You gonna Succeed like Michael Air Jordan, Will Smith and Co.

And it's not by accident because Aesthetic is a part of our hu(e)man *(hue = dark - man = race)* kind ever since, we were on the planet. All you need to do is to love your **"Self"** kind and start to study life by reading books, by trying to get in touch with superior people, who live a certain aesthetic apart from normal -expectation- Piggy Pink *(their history is written in blood all over the planet and stored in several archives around the globe)* Kind.

Piggy Pink People *(their history is written in blood all over the planet and stored in several archives around the globe)* see us as their enemy and Beautiful Brown Hu*(e)*man *(hue = dark - man = race)* Beings see them as equal ever since these d-evils entered Africa. But a lot of us do not wanna use the word enemy for the Piggy Pink d-evil race *(their history is written in blood all over the planet and stored in several archives around the globe)*, because of these 95er *(95% are Uncle Toms)*, are afraid to stand up and fight. Everything that walks everything that crawls, everything that flies, -it has an enemy.

The rats have an enemy, a mosquito, a mouse, a bird, everything on planet earth has a natural enemy. We have to understand this.

When I say enemy, I know definitely that the race who started to label themselves as **"White"** is for centuries our oppressor. - factz! However, we have become unconscious of that sort of proven fact that he the d-evil never did anything well to our African Descent Community. There is no doubt about it because *his history is written in blood and archived around the globe*. Ignorance in the 95er Community. - *(95% are Uncle Toms)* - " Before you come to tell that you know 3 Piggy Pinks, who are completely different, I want you to challenge your cracker @ home, with that simple yes or no answer: "Would you change position to be **"BLACK!"** If he/she does not say yes or no immediately and needs to stutter around, you know which penis - slave master penis you suckin' during nighttime.

In the animal world, there is no mistake who his real enemy is. If a creature stands in front of a lion, he knows immediately by nature, he needs to run as quickly as he can or otherwise he is going to end up dead.

What we need to do is: Stop working for them. Dancing for them. Acting for them, marrying them, sleeping with them, and worshipping them. Once we stop that we will be on our way to the Kingdom of Aesthetic.

Piggy Pink People has created what we are
(**"BLACKS"**) and the majority of us conform to how
the world views us. As long we stay in Piggy Pink *(their
history is written in blood all over the planet and stored in several archives
around the globe)* People Racial Racist Paradise, we can
never become as a community fully the people we can
potentially be. We still hold on to Piggy Pink People
(*their history is written in blood all over the planet and stored in several
archives around the globe)* Racial Racist Paradise that they are
from the better **"White Race."**
If the police pull you over while you are driving, he is
not a single second confused that you as an African are
his enemy. He is willing to pull his gone and firer a
bullet into your body. - That simple. The police officer
knows who you are, he understands that there is a
strange history between the d-evil and African-Race. He
knows you have the potential to be the best on the
planet and that makes you become his enemy. The d-
evil understands exactly who Beautiful Brown
Hu*(e)*man *(hue = dark - man = race)* Beings are, this is why he
keeps his foot on our necks. The d-evil makes sure that
everything, we can try to present in an aesthetic context,
he tries to condemn that.

I got pulled over, back in those days all the time. Just because I had a damn Porsche and I was not supposed to drive such a car as a Beautiful Brown Human Being.

Police Officer: "Nigger, what the hell are you doing in this car?" I got pulled over during a week of seven days five times. Even I was driving normal speed limit and taking my time, but when the -Blue -Klux - Clan saw me, they see an enemy that is someone who has the potential to wake up because you need to understand as long the African lion is asleep, like all the damn 95er (95% are Uncle Toms), they can enslave us, they can cash us financially out, they can seduce us by women who pretend to need an LV, Prada, Chanel, Versace, Gucci and all these other fake racist brands.

Chapter 18

Pattern of the 95er *(95% are Uncle Toms)*

They do understand and see what is going on. But they act in a context of ignorance. They do not necessarily deny the reality of the evil Piggy Pink Race as it is more than to get something so-called better. It starts with what is good hair and not so good hair, it developed into smelly wigs/weaves. Then, the journey takes places not to date within the African Community, because no matter what Piggy Pink has done to that individual of an Uncle Tom - *Piggy Pink he/she is considered the better choice because if a Baby comes around that child is going to have a different skin complexion Uncle Tom people are going to conform to all those racist rules:*

"Yes, Master racism does not exist, it's just a creation out of my fantasy. Yes, Master, it is our own African Descent fault that the condition we are in is our own creation." - by contributing a Baby to the Piggy Pink world is the first step to be acknowledged by the so-called **"Superior White Society."** Uncle Tom is going to receive full acceptance if that Baby grows up and of course, is telling such none sense - Actually, Africans are not my type to date. At the same time being aware, one part in the family has a darker skin complexion - he/she pushes her mother away- she receives a Baby by a Piggy Pink *(their history is written in blood all over the planet and stored in several archives around the globe)* , that enters the world as to be seen as **"White."** The Baby is going to grow up in a Piggy Pink Racist environment, where nobody ever would consider referring the N-Word to him/her. That child is going to marry a Piggy Pink *(their history is written in blood all over the planet and stored in several archives around the globe)* and the Grandmother can be proud of because she contributed a racist to Piggy Pink *(their history is written in blood all over the planet and stored in several archives around the globe)* society that is fully accepted.

George Zimmerman his Grandmother was from African Descent. **When he killed that young African-American he claimed during the trial:** "I can't be a racist, my grandmother is "BLACK!"

Seriously, how proud must an Uncle Tom feel, when she/he was able to contribute over several generations a fully accepted Piggy Pink baby and that grandchild was willing to Kill an African-American Boy, 11 years younger than Mr. Zimmerman and get away with it.

The Grandmother reached the goal of being fully accepted by contributing a child to Piggy Pink society, he is fully seen as a Piggy Pink and acts like a hidden racist to kill African-Americans. - Good job & the Oscar goes to the African-Descent grandmother of George Zimmer (age 28 years)! - thank you very much for contributing, this racist to our unaesthetic world.

Are Uncle Tom People out of their natural mind?
Well, let me explain it to you with a very graphic
example:

Imagine a circus where a bear rides a bicycle. The bear is not in his natural environment, he does not really wanna sit on a bicycle. Because the bear is told what to do we consider him out of his natural mind. At the same time, we understand he does not know better yet. If the bear wakes up one day and goes to the director (Piggy Pink) to let him go: "I wanna be able to dress like you, to live where you live, I wanna be able to eat what you eat. The director (Piggy Pink) is going to say: "Well, you must be out of your mind." The bear did not ask to go back to his natural environment he asked to be seen as equal as his director (Piggy Pink).
What do we learn from that story?

Answer: *As long Piggy Pink has a certain control of our aesthetic spirit as a slave master, as seeing us as liquid money, as a sexual object, prostitute or sugar baby, niggers, thugs, we need to ride the bike the way he wants us to sit on that vehicle.*

Another example:

...when we were told in the United States we were free, in our demand for freedom, we wanted to live where Piggy Pink People live, we wanted to eat what these unhealthy looking racist people eat, we wanted to dress the same way the former slave master dressed. We wanted to have the same hair the slave master had. Basically, we wanted to have what Piggy Pink got. So we clearly demonstrated that we are clearly out of our natural mind.

Because in our demand for freedom, we never demanded anything connected within our own historical Beautiful Brown Hu(e)man (hue = dark - man = race) *Beings - Aesthetic - - African-Foundation. It means we are operating, still operating with the consciousness created by Piggy Pink* **(their history is written in blood all over the planet and stored in several archives around the globe)** *Supremacy. We are operating, with a self-destructive consciousness created by Piggy Pink People* **(their history is written in blood all over the planet and stored in several archives around the globe).**
So, again the questions are Uncle Toms out of their mind?

We need to re-connect with our own aesthetic cultural-foundation rooted in the universal understanding and concepts.

Chapter 19

What does the Aesthetic really believe in? We follow the teaching of our true Ancient African Descent history. We do not refer to ourselves as **"BLACKS"**, **"N!GGERS"**, **"NEGROES"** all these foolish words is a creation by the pinkish looking race, who gave themselves the label **"WHITE"** and in reality, they are far away from that colour. Furthermore, these people still telling us we are not lovable Hu*(e)*man *(hue = dark - man = race)* Beings of African Descent.

As members of the Aesthetic, we dedicate our life to teach our brothaz&sistaz who they really are, what the d-evil is never going to teach them. We from the aesthetic world understand that the present generation is not different from those racists from the past.

We have been robbed from our Beautiful Africa, we have been robbed from our language, our culture, our deeper spiritual personality. We have been giving such names as Jones, Smith, Miller, Robinson, Green, Little.... what has nothing to do with ourselves as Beautiful Brown Hu*(e)*man *(hue = dark - man = race)* Beings of African Descent. Some racist has robbed us of our land and our ancient culture and erase from us that which is our by our nature.

Today we are very disoriented people and treated all around the world as if we are "BLACK-DIRT", "FILTHY-N!GGERS," "UNEDUCATED NEGROES FROM AMERICA," "SAGGING THUGZ" and the list goes on and on!

The Europeans have been brought up with a Piggy Pink Supremacy *(their history is written in blood all over the planet and stored in several archives around the globe)* mentality, they do not know, where their culture comes from, they think there is not the much bigger thing, then this Pinky Pink skin complexion.

They like to see us dancing, cooning and acting like fools. Please, Piggy Pink *(their history is written in blood all over the planet and stored in several archives around the globe)* study your ancient history, who gave you roads and a form of civilization? When the Piggy Pink race was living in caves in Europe, we Africans were dressed in silk and had a civilized culture ruling from Egypt to today's South Africa.

And if Piggy Pink *(their history is written in blood all over the planet and stored in several archives around the globe)* study their history, they mostly start with the Romans. The romans say, they got their civilization based on the teaching by the Greeks. And if you go to study, what the Greeks say Pythagoras and his followers, these Greeks say that they got their knowledge from the Egyptians. Question: Who are the true Egyptians? The real name of Egypt is Camit! The meaning of Camit is: The land of the dark hu*(e)*man race *(hue = dark - man = race)*

Everything Piggy Pink *(their history is written in blood all over the planet and stored in several archives around the globe)* is today, is an inspiration from Africa. We were stupid enough to give it to them. We educated them, we taught them science, mathematics and civilization. How do these Piggy Pink *(their history is written in blood all over the planet and stored in several archives around the globe)* treat us in return? They wanna teach the whole world that they went to Africa and found Beautiful Brown Hu*(e)*man *(hue = dark - man = race)* Beings of African Descent with a bone in our nose. Swinging from one tree to another bigger stable tree. They wanna make us believe that they did us Beautiful Brown Hu*(e)*man Beings *(hue = dark - man = race)* a favour. Piggy Pink *(their history is written in blood all over the planet and stored in several archives around the globe)* is a damn liar.

The Aesthetic represents a learning class of Beautiful Brown Hu*(e)*man *(hue = dark - man = race)* Beings of African Descent. We are a part of the conscious community that is why they could not handle brotha Malcolm X, that is why these **"Whites"** sent Uncle Toms to kill brotha Malcolm. Malcolm was not speaking some foolishness, while he was slowly decoding Piggy Pink racism and Uncle Tom behaviour, he was speaking total truth based on historical factz.

We from the Aesthetic are going to challenge Uncle Toms *(95% are Uncle Toms)* and Piggy Pink *(their history is written in blood all over the planet and stored in several archives around the globe)* to show us by facts only that we are wrong.

We are like New Kids on the block. When it comes to an institution to decode Piggy Pink racism from the inside. We only deal with the truth. Our brothaz and sistaz will know the truth and the truth shall set them free. That is what the teaching of the Aesthetic is all about. We can prove what we say, we challenge Piggy Pink *(their history is written in blood all over the planet and stored in several archives around the globe)* and Uncle Toms *(95% are Uncle Toms)* can you back up your knowledge?

Pink Pink *(their history is written in blood all over the planet and stored in several archives around the globe)* gave Jesus blue eyes and blond hair, but all other scriptures say, he had hair like lamb wool. Do they wanna let people believe in Jesus or do they wanna make us worship **"White Supremacy."** We from the Aesthetic believe that we can have our own spiritual Lord of righteousness, we believe, that we have the right to teach our children, the way we wanna teach them. We believe that we should have manufactured industries, where we can manufacture our own Haute Couture, our own goods, our own material, we believe, that you should go out of Africa. Stop destabilizing African governments. We believe that you should stop rubbing our minerals from Africa. We believe that freedom, justice and equality that every hu*(e)*man *(hue = dark - man = race)* being has the right to self-determination.

We believe based on the damage your ancestors inflicted on my ancestors that the d-evil must pay reparations. The Germans right now pay the Jews *(Jewish people consider "Blacks" as liquid money) = (racist people pay racist people)*. Sadam Hussain is liable for reparations, what he did to the Kuwaitis in the so-called war: "Dessert storm." The American government is paying Japanese reparations. But if we people from African Descent mention reparations for 400 years of the most brutal treatment in the history of the world, Uncle Tom *(95% are Uncle Toms)* and Piggy Pink *(their history is written in blood all over the planet and stored in several archives around the globe)* this is some kind of a joke. And how dare we as Africans speak in this kind of manner. Well, this is what we believe as members of the Aesthetic. We invite any of you Uncle Tom and Piggy Pink *(their history is written in blood all over the planet and stored in several archives around the globe)* to dispute what we say. We invite any of you to disproof the truth.

Every time we develop a leader that lead us from the darkness to the holy land, they get killed, they get sent to prison, they get deported because Piggy Pink *(their history is written in blood all over the planet and stored in several archives around the globe)* is so terrified of another power that will stand up and fight the injustice by Piggy Pink *(their history is written in blood all over the planet and stored in several archives around the globe)*.

They do not wanna see such a leader. As long we are some effeminate, freakish, caricature of a **"BLACK MAN"** they will pay us little money and put us on Television. If we rap filth about our women, and smoke dope and do all kinds of negativity, Piggy Pink *(their history is written in blood all over the planet and stored in several archives around the globe)* will promote that. But if we decide, we wanna be upright/upstanding people, self-respecting, they gonna have a problem with that. We intend to establish a government on our own. We wanna form a brotha-hood first among our own. Sista-hood among our women. We intend to re-integrate our African family because the **"BLACK FAMILY"** has been disintegrated. The corner stone of an aesthetic empire is family. Husband - Wive & Child. That is the most powerful unit in the universe. That unity has been destroyed by Piggy Pink *(their history is written in blood all over the planet and stored in several archives around the globe)* People when slavery started. And now many of our women are a single parent raising these children, by themselves. We intend to put a stop on that. We intend to command respect because we have self-respect.

If you Piggy Pink *(their history is written in blood all over the planet and stored in several archives around the globe)* and Uncle Tom *(95% are Uncle Toms)* have a problem with that, that is fine and leave us forever alone. Our weapon is the truth and the back-up is your racist history that is written in blood around the globe.

We need to stop looking outside our community for help. We need to stop to look for a Piggy Pink to help us.

Where does the healing come from? You cut yourself - where does the healing come from? **Answer:** It comes from deep within our own self-body. All of the raw materials that you need to heal yourself is within ourselves. So if the African Community needs healing, where do we get the healing from? It has to come within ourselves. -And we can do that.

Brothaz and sistaz our open enemy works on our differences as a tool to set us apart from what we really are. That is how he was able to step into Africa and divide us from one another. The d-d-evil goes into the family to divide the husband against the wife, the wife against the husband, the children against their father. We must break these barriers down.

The true value of our women. Many of our brothaz and sistaz do not have a concept of the value of a sophisticated sistaz, that if she acts like a true lady, she is the backbone of our empire. I wanna stress I do not talk bitches the opposite of a thug. What I mean a woman who understands like a gentleman, what it means to step back all the time, whether to do a reflection or to avoid strange situations for the future. I do not talk morally fallen down women, who dress expansive and do not understand the language of the upscale aristocracy world. Furthermore, I do not talk these African descent old fashion mothers, who beat up their children and later ask for an apology, based on the fact, these children are grown-ups and able to fight back. As a perfect example when I say true lady of African Descent: Michelle Obama!" She is the backbone of Barack, who would never yell around publicly or do other strange ghetto things or morally fallen engagements. Man and women today have no true concept what a woman really is and a great value of a woman. How can we prove it? **Well, the earth we are standing on is never referred to in a masculine way (mother earth - mother nature). It is always something feminine. Even the universe is a -SHE- and never an -ITS- or something else. The universe gave birth to all planets and mother earth gave birth to all lives. Mother earth is where all hueman kind comes from. This where all our food comes from. This is where all our materials come from.**

All of it comes from the earth. Having disrespect from the earth that we get everything from, what would that say about such a person? That individual is very ignorant or very ungrateful. Because, if the earth provides us with everything, why would you then disrespect the earth. The Lady is to be seen as something holy as the earth *(I stress Lady and not girl trash)*. Especially, the Lady of African descent is to be treated as something special, based on the fact the society is full of Piggy Pink *(their history is written in blood all over the planet and stored in several archives around the globe)* racism. She is extremely important for the right development of the next generation. Without her, we can't grow valuable hu*(e)*man *(hue = dark - man = race)* beings. The true Lady is so important as a backbone in our African-Descent society, as Michelle Obama for Barack. Because, without such a great Lady, there will be no greater children. The African-Descent Lady is a fancy, emotional, creation of the Lord based on the fact she is able to give birth to all skin-complexion on planet earth. She is the mystery of our true African spirit. Her genes are worth as diamonds or gold from Africa. Because everything that comes directly from her is purely aesthetic and must not be destroyed by the environment of Piggy Pink Supremacy *(their history is written in blood all over the planet and stored in several archives around the globe)*.

The Caucasian world is built on a big bluff, but understand these people work only on a clever equation. However, they do not have the inner entirety of deep inner knowledge nor that six sense, what you have if your skin complexion is dark enough.

The African lady is so important and significant for the next generation that both child and mother need to be guarded, she is to be formed in a diamond to teach as the first teacher of her child, knowledge & wisdom. We need to develop the woman in a lady.

Author: If you are a woman check your value system. The clothes you are wearing.

If she has no substance of deeper wisdom and knowledge for the next generation, get rid of her immediately, your aesthetic time on planet earth is short and too valuable.

They want us to love them? We from the Aesthetic will never love our oppressors. We are Beautiful Brown Hu*(e)*man Being *(hue = dark - man = race)* of African Descent with a deeper six sense of spirituality. Where is the humanity of Piggy Pink People *(their history is written in blood all over the planet and stored in several archives around the globe)*? towards our brothaz and sistaz? When did they show as a group humanity? Yes, they say we are **"BLACK"** Hu*(e)*man *(hue = dark - man = race)* beings? When did they recognize that? Was it after they wrote in the American institution, that we are only 3/5 of a hu*(e)*man being *(hue = dark - man = race)*? Was it while we were slaves? Was it while they were showing us on TV dead and stiff - **"BLACK -AFRICANS?"** - with flies in a mouth? Is that the situation they consider us a hu*(e)*man *(hue = dark - man = race)* Being? When did I become a hu*(e)*man *(hue = dark - man = race)* Being in your eyes? We will never love Piggy Pink People *(their history is written in blood all over the planet and stored in several archives around the globe)*. Until they prove that they are no more devils. So far, we have not seen any significant change in the African-Descent world that shows true humanity from Piggy Pink *their history is written in blood all over the planet and stored in several archives around the globe)*. We from the Aesthetic will never step back from the truth of the evil Piggy Pink *(their history is written in blood all over the planet and stored in several archives around the globe)* race. Because we know what we are dealing with.

But I am different because my wife/husband is **"BLACK!"** Well, very nice words! Look @ the situation our continent is in. Native Beautiful Brown Hu(e)man *(hue = dark - man =race)* Beings of African Descent are living in townships, while Piggy Pink *(their history is written in blood all over the planet and stored in several archives around the globe)* Racist are living in high-rise luxury in OUR HOME CONTINENT AFRICA.

Our brothaz and sistaz in Africa living in a ghetto on drugs and alcohol provided by the devil. While they live on Bonday Beach in high-rise luxury. Even in these days in India the same thing. Everywhere you go on the planet same thing. So until you do justice by taking action to give us reparation, you are not required to love our LADIES I stress _lady_ and not bitches or sexual arrangements in a *(fantasy bubble)*. Freedom, justice, and equality among ourselves. We live in a time where we recognize that we need to love us first, our skin complexion, come together to unify and learn from one another under one roof of Beautiful Brown Hu*(e)*man Beings *(hue = dark - man = race)*

Chapter 20

The Aesthetic is a tool to let us stop drinking alcohol, the Aesthetic is a tool, that let us stop abusing our women, the Aesthetic is a tool, that let us take charge of everything and educate your Beautiful Brown Hu*(e)*man *(hue = dark - man = race)* Being child only by people of African Descent *(not those 95% Uncle Toms)*, the Aesthetic is a tool, that teaches you to completely submit your life to the aestheticism. Do not worship me as the author of this book submit only to the will of an aesthetic life.

The Arabs won't come to give **"BLACKS"** any advice, the Chinese people are not gonna come around to give **"BLACKS"** any advice, and the number one enemy is never going to come to fix our **"BLACK"** problems.

Post-Slavery syndrome. We have all our ideas and experiences, what we have to experience having a Beautiful Brown Skin Complexion. We still have these 95er *(95% are Uncle Toms)* and these few percentage terms of mainly Gentleman, who are educated about slavery, Piggy Pink Supremacy *(their history is written in blood all over the planet and stored in several archives around the globe)*. It is not a feeling thing it is a cerebral thing. For that person who lives in this skin, it is personal. I am the Author of the book - How to destroy & decode racism - I am absolute sensitive ever since I was a child, I could never understand these 95er *(95% are uncle Toms)* who walk away from our deep inner African beauty to worship rather an ugly, unhealthy looking d-evil. As I grew older I understood the social race ladder and the creation of the d-evil. I thank the lord that he let me enter the world as a none 95er *(95% are Uncle Toms)*. If we look @ the fundamental construction of trauma and if we understand trauma from the multi-generational perspective. For example, Jewish holocaust, the fact is that this particular group is very clear about honouring the holocaust that Spielberg is going to make another movie. These people are conscious to ensure that generations will come, will never forget, the Holocaust and more important its impact upon the religious group of Jewish people. But if we look @ African holocaust, there always is: Come on it's been a long time ago, we are not racist, when slavery took place you were not even born, not all Piggy Pink *(their history is written in blood all over the planet and stored in several archives around the globe)* are evil, I know few **"BLACKS"** their Piggy Pink partners are good (Masters ;-) ...)! You get so much push back when you discuss that topic, within the African Descent Community and within of course the racist dominant Society.

Let's break the legacy of slavery down by putting these layers back of Piggy Pink People *(their history is written in blood all over the planet and stored in several archives around the globe)*. This message goes mainly to you 95er *(95% are Uncle Toms)* do not double check it with your Piggy Pink Fucker *(their history is written in blood all over the planet and stored in several archives around the globe)*, please go to the central archive in Washington, New York or London, take 14 days off from your work and I swear to you the truth has been written down by your considered "BETTER RACE!"

Post-slavery syndrome trauma follows trauma created by Piggy Pink People *(their history is written in blood all over the planet and stored in several archives around the globe)* only. You can have 246 years of post-slavery trauma if they were **"White"** they were unaffected. Everybody who has a slavery background has been affected and infected by this thing called post-slavery syndrome. That is the part that might get uncomfortable. That really shows the elephant in the room. The most important thing is to recognize it, that the next generation can heal. We must understand, this is not a process that anybody can heal individually. This is a collective process. Everybody can experience a single trauma indirectly you do not have to be present in the room. We take 9/11 as our guide example: A lady in the building wanted to step out of the building, but the security guard forbids her to escape: "Stay where you are!" She jumped over the security guard to escape. - *you need to understand the building did not collapse yet.* There were people watching on the TV, what was going while drinking beer, - not traumatized. There were people for example in Brazil, in mental psychological help following everything on TV, - on medication maybe.

The various how everybody is traumatized is different. So, when we discuss post-traumatic slavery, we do not talk about one trauma. We do not lead a conversation about a specific location or event when slavery took place.

We are talking about generations of trauma. With no psychological medical help by a professional. What I know about sugar plantations, what I know about American slavery, there was no medical or psychological help when the slave master who considered **"BLACKS"** as products, raped a female slave. After slavery was officially over, there was no therapy available for African Americans. Nobody came to support us mentally, well, we know, what you have been through, we know it was rough ... etc! After slavery ended officially *(French, Americans, Portuguese, English)* the trauma continued for people of African Descent.

Well, we do the math-science: Hundred of years of slavery = trauma no treatment. Liberated = still traumatized no treatment. No equal rights = trauma no treatment. The bottom line, it did not end and has not ended yet. We have been living so far without any professional help by our oppressors. The journey I gonna take you on gives a deeper perspective what

Piggy Pink *(their history is written in blood all over the planet and stored in several archives around the globe)* post slavery really is. And clinical, what is post-traumatic stress disorder? What does it look like? What is a post-traumatic disorder? The difficulty of falling or staying asleep, hyper-vigilant, these are symptoms of a post-traumatic disorder. Example: Great-grandmother, who was a slave got treated well by slave master while her sista getting raped every Sunday after the slave master came back from church. Only her sista yells around all the time when a Piggy Pink is in the room. The sista plays as usual 95er *(95% are uncle Toms)*: "But he is o.k., I know few sistaz who get along with him well." Her raped sista has even problems to fall asleep. No, professional psychological help no back-up help by her sista because she is a classical 95er *(95% are Uncle Toms)* - my Piggy Pink is different and additionally I know 3 "BLACKS" with a Piggy Pink - they are just wonderful. The none raped sista 95er *(95% are Uncle Toms)* have not witnessed such a trauma, but what are they learning? Do they learn to stay away from Piggy Pink *(their history is written in blood all over the planet and stored in several archives around the globe)* and help to decode the devil?

The answer is very simple: NO! The **"WHITE"** race is the goal to achieve to be seen as equal.

Piggy Pink *(their history is written in blood all over the planet and stored in several archives around the globe)* post slavery really is. And clinical, what is post-traumatic stress disorder? What does it look like? What is a post-traumatic disorder? The difficulty of falling or staying asleep, hyper-vigilant, these are symptoms of a post-traumatic disorder. Example: Great-grandmother, who was a slave got treated well by slave master while her sista getting raped every Sunday after the slave master came back from church. Only her sista yells around all the time when a Piggy Pink is in the room. The sista plays as usual 95er *(95% are uncle Toms)*: "But he is o.k., I know few sistaz who get along with him well." Her raped sista has even problems to fall asleep. No, professional psychological help no back-up help by her sista because she is a classical 95er *(95% are Uncle Toms)* - my Piggy Pink is different and additionally I know 3 **"BLACKS"** with a **"WHITE"** - they are just wonderful. The none raped sista 95er *(95% are Uncle Toms)* have not witnessed such a trauma, but what are they learning? Do they learn to stay away from Piggy Pink *(their history is written in blood all over the planet and stored in several archives around the globe)* and help to decode the devil? The answer is very simple: NO! The "WHITE" race is the goal to achieve to be seen as equal.

James Madison
1809 - 1817
President of the
United States

He was a very important figure in American History.
He said: "Blacks are inhabitants, but debased by
servitude below equal level of free inhabitants.
The true state of the case is that they partake of both
these qualities: being considered by our laws, in
some respects, as persons, and in other respects as
property.... This is, in fact, their true character. It is
the character bestowed on them by the laws under
which they live, and it will not be denied that these
are the proper criterion."

The system of "justice" developed under the U.S. Constitution was dedicated to providing the legal basis for complete control of the slave master over their human property.

"Being considered by our laws, in some respects, as persons, and in other respects as property" which meant they could be put on an auction block to be bought and sold, and witness their loved ones taken from them as someone else's purchase.

"It is the character bestowed on them by the laws under which they live"—which meant they could be forced to work like animals under the whip, chained up and hounded by dogs if they dared to escape; subjected to subhuman conditions of life, and the constant knowledge that the slave master could end their lives on even the slightest whim.

Piggy Pink Southerners *(their history is written in blood all over the planet and stored in several archives around the globe)* who enjoyed the slaves and their "BLACK SEXUAL MISTRESSES" - *(name it house slaves or Uncle Tom women)* wanted to count their slaves. But how to count slaves? James Madison: "Well, you can't really count them, because they are not hu*(e)*man *(hue = dark - man = race)* Beings. But slavery ended therefore we need to give them the option of 3/5 of a hueman Being." As a result "BLACKS were countable in numbers!"

Richard Oswald
1705 - 1784

The son of a Presbyterian Minister.
International trader of enslaved Africans. Majority shareholder in Oswald & Co.
Fortune in todays money $ 68 millions.

What is so deep about this Piggy Pink *(their history is written in blood all over the planet and stored in several archives around the globe)* is the fact how wealthy he became. Base on the fact he was a slave trader. Also, we should not forget, that his family in these days still benefit from those days, when we were not considered hu*(e)*man *(hue = dark - man = race)* beings.

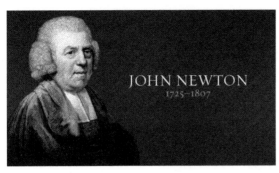

Reverend
John Newton
1725 - 1807
Author of the
gospel song:
Amazing Grace

"Slaves are lesser creatures without a Christian soul and then not destined for the next world.

How could people who deem themselves superior, who see themselves as the civilizers, who recognize themselves as what Uncle Tom (95% are Uncle Toms) *consider as the manifest destiny, how do they reconcile, bag and engaging in barbaric behaviour? Hand in Hand with this mindset and although in today's time, if we deal with Uncle Toms* (95% are Uncle Toms), *it is so damaging. I call it a secret: "How many brothaz and sistaz are in mental psychiatric help? Isn't it the secret that makes us sick? How long have Piggy Pink* (their history is written in blood all over the planet and stored in several archives around the globe) *that secret? How many generations had the son to keep the secret that his grandfather was a big-time racist?*

Carl Von Linnaeus
1707-1778
A scientist???

He developed a system based on skin color as a race classification tool. He is the inventor of color criteria for "BLACKS"

Homo Americans: *Native Americans. They are red (actually they are brown) , colaeric, abstinent, and regulated by custom.*

Homo Europeans: *White (their real color is Piggy Pink) blue eyed gentle and govern by laws.*

Homo Asiaticus: *as sallow, grave, dignified, avaricious, and ruled by opinions*

Home Afer: *Black (the true skin color is brown or dark brown) phlegmatic, cunning, lazy, careless, and govern by caprice.*

Johann Friedrich
Blumenbach
1752 - 1804

He originated the term
Caucasian.

He took the term
Caucasian for the
science from the

mount Caucasus. Because he considered in that area
the most beautiful people on planet earth.

Johann Friedrich Blumenbach: "For in the first place
the stock we have seen, the most beautiful form of the
skull, from which , as we mean and primeval type, the
others diverge by most easy gradations on both sides
to the two ultimate extremes *(that is, on the one side the
Mongolian on the other Ethiopian)*. Besides it is white in
colour, which we may fairly assume to have been the
primitive colour of mankind."

Basically, he is saying the world began *"White!"*

Thomas Jefferson 1743 - 1826
3rd President of the United States of America
& slave owner

Thomas Jefferson: "Blacks smell bad and are physically unattractive, they require less sleep, they are dump, cowardly and inappeasable of feelings grief advance it therefore as a suspicion only...blacks whether originally a distinct race or made distinct by time and circumstances, are inferior to the whites in the endowments of body and mind.
Thomas Jefferson fathered slaves. - *so she could not smell that bad.*
You need to understand he is highly regarded in the United States. There are more status in Washington of him than anybody ever had in America.
Do we have anywhere in the world **a statue of Adolf Hitler?**

James Marion Sims

1813 - 1883
Doctor

He reasoned that slaves were able to bear great pain because their race made them more durable, and thus they were well suited for painful medical experimentation.

This man would just cut into the vagina of a woman with a knife. More important is what he did to infants.

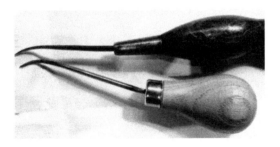

He would use a shoemaker's awl and stick that into the head of a new born infant.

In order to re-adjust their skulls. Of course there was a 100% death rate. The reason that he could do it: "BLACKS are not hu*(e)*man *(hue = dark - man = race)*, they are properties, they can't feel pain. That is what all those of Piggy Pink race *(their history is written in blood all over the planet and stored in several archives around the globe)* still believe in these days. We can not feel pain.

Rape Law in the United States

No "WHITE" *(actually Piggy Pink)* could ever rape a slave woman. The regulations of Law, as to the "WHITE" race, on the subject of sexual intercourse do not and can not, for obvious reasons, apply to slaves, their intercourse is promiscuous.
Piggy Pink *(their history is written in blood all over the planet and stored in several archives around the globe)*: We are not raping them, they are by nature not Hu(e)man Beings *(hue = dark - man = race)*. They are promiscuous.

Psychology of rape: The fact that Piggy Pink *(their history is written in blood all over the planet and stored in several archives around the globe)* men could profit from raping their female slaves does not mean that the motive was economical. The rape of slave women by their masters was primarily a weapon of terror that reinforced **"White"** domination over their Hu*(e)*man *(hue = dark - man = race)* property. Rape was an act of physical violence designed to stifle **"BLACK"** women's will to resist and to remind them of their servile status.

The casual killing act: Virginia Statute 1705

If any slave resist his master or owner or another person by his or her order correcting such slaves and wil happen to be killed in such correction it shall not be counted Ellary, but the master, owner, and every other person so giving correction, shall be quit of all punishment and accusation for the same, as if such accident had never happened.
-That means if you correcting someone and beat him to death Piggy Pink *(their history is written in blood all over the planet and stored in several archives around the globe)* was backed up by the law no to feel any guilt. Piggy Pink women beat African American children to death. You need to understand " it was not her fault she was just correcting him."

Misdiagnosing the mind

In the early years of the nineteenth century, a physician named Samuel A. Cartwright argued that two particular forms of mental illness, caused by mental disorders, were prevalent among slaves. One was drapetomania, which was diagnosable by a single symptom: The uncontrollable urge to escape from slavery.

- What Piggy Pink *(their history is written in blood all over the planet and stored in several archives around the globe)* has basically done is to pathologist your need to be free. "Must be something wrong with him, keeps trying to free himself."

The lynching in America of African Americans happened after slavery. Not during slavery. Because this is a reaction of Piggy Pink "White" fear *(their history is written in blood all over the planet and stored in several archives around the globe)*. So they founded the Ku-Klux-Klan. Today they do not wear costumes anymore, they wear uniforms - cops killing blacks! Please, watch the picture above. The little girl is witnessing everything that a man who is not considered a human being gets killed. Her body language shows that she is not disturbed by that. She is the impact for the next generation, who is going to teach her children **"Blacks are not humans!"** As a grown-up she is going to feel zero empathy for **"BLACKS"** - because we are not hu*(e)*man *(hue = dark - man = race)* beings. Whatever she saw and was taught socialize to believe, makes him who is hanging from the tree no longer a Beautiful Brown Hu*(e)*man Being *(hue = dark - man = race)*.

That is the greatest danger to Piggy Pink *(their history is written in blood all over the planet and stored in several archives around the globe)* is that they can't feel it. There is a reason why Piggy Pink *(their history is written in blood all over the planet and stored in several archives around the globe)* can't feel what we are talking about.

Piggy Pink and Uncle Tom collectively: Come on it's all over now, that was the past, not every **"WHITE"** is the same.

Please Mr. Piggy Pink *(their history is written in blood all over the planet and stored in several archives around the globe)* and all you 95er *(95% are Uncle Toms)* who has something sexually going on with a Piggy Pink Racist (their history is written in blood all over the planet and stored in several archives around the globe) do me a favour and say that to a JEW!

Lightning Source UK Ltd.
Milton Keynes UK
UKHW05f1136010818
326614UK00009B/174/P

9 781389 553714